P.E.E.R.

A Practical Approach to Project Management, leadership, and growing your business.

By Michael Drapala

© 2026 Michael Drapala

All rights reserved.

No part of this book may be reproduced, distributed, or transmitted in any form or by any means, including photocopying, recording, or other electronic or mechanical methods, without the prior written permission of the author, except in the case of brief quotations embodied in critical reviews and specific other noncommercial uses permitted by copyright law.

For permission requests, contact:

Email: mdrapala17@gmail.com

Website: www.linkoutreach.org

Table of Contents:

PART I: PLAN
Vision………………………………………………………………8
Problem Identification………..………………………………12
Target Population………………..…………………………………17
Partners………………………………………………………………21
Resources……………………………………………………………25
Risks & Mitigation……………………………………………………29
Timeline…………………………………………………………….33

PART II: ESTABLISH
The Goal…………………………………………………………..39
Staffing & Volunteer Needs……………………………………….....42
Communication Plan…………………………………………………46
Physical Space ……………………………………………………51
Safety Planning……………………………………………………54

PART III: ELEVATE
What's Working…………………………………………………...60
What's Not Working………………………………………………64
Feedback…………………………………………………………68
Barriers……………………………………………………………72
Next-Step Growth Actions……………………………………...76

PART IV: REVIEW
Additional Feedback Review……………………………………82
Participant Follow-Up…………………………………………...86
Benchmark Data & Reporting……………………………………...90
The Last R… Repeat……………………………………………95

Acknowledgments

To my Nana, whose quiet strength shaped the foundation of who I am. Her gentleness, wisdom, and steady example continue to guide me every day.

To my wife Julia, whose unwavering support, patience, and belief in me turned long nights into possibilities and challenges into momentum. Your encouragement made this book and every dream behind it possible.

To my daughters, Maddie and Kylie, who remind me why growth matters. Your curiosity, humor, and resilience inspire me to build better systems, lead with compassion, and leave a world that is just a little easier for the next generation to navigate.

To Curtis Warren and Latisha Brossard, who provided me with such outstanding mentorship and fully believed in me. You both have been my rocks professionally and spiritually. My love for program management and helping people was born and deepened by your unwavering, continued support.

Foreword

In every successful business, nonprofit, or community program, there comes a moment when leaders must confront the fact that good intentions and hard work are not enough. Programs succeed when they have structure, clarity, and a consistent rhythm for growth. They fail when those elements are missing, no matter how enthusiastic the team may be. That reality is what makes the P.E.E.R. model so valuable.

P.E.E.R.: Plan, Establish, Elevate, Review, is a simple, repeatable system designed to strengthen programs by strengthening the people who run them. It strips away unnecessary complexity and provides leaders with a process they can rely on in any environment. Whether a program is being built from scratch or is struggling to find momentum, P.E.E.R. offers a practical, accessible, and most importantly, sustainable framework.

What sets P.E.E.R. apart is that it was not created in a boardroom or imagined in a textbook. It grew from my lived experiences. I have spent more than a decade leading programs in environments where real people, real needs, and absolute pressure shaped every decision.

For over ten years, I have served in leadership roles that required coordination, crisis management, team building, and program development. My journey includes:

- Founding nonprofit organizations from the ground up
- Serving inside established nonprofits, helping strengthen their structures
- Guiding teams through change, conflict, and growth
- Building support systems for vulnerable populations
- Designing and improving programs where follow-through meant everything.

These experiences taught me that programs thrive not because of complicated theories, but because leaders commit to a straightforward process: setting direction, establishing structure, elevating their people, and consistently reviewing.

The P.E.E.R. model brings that real-world wisdom into a format any leader can use.

Businesses benefit from P.E.E.R. because it creates alignment among vision and action, people and goals, and leadership and execution. Programs benefit because they bring order to chaos and rhythm to growth. Nonprofits benefit because they provide structure for missions that rely on limited resources and high levels of trust. And leaders benefit because they help build teams that can operate confidently and independently.

In this book, you will find not only a framework, but also the mindset behind it, the belief that programs succeed when people succeed. My approach is grounded in patience, clarity, and the power of consistent improvement. Through setbacks, successes, and years of firsthand leadership, I have refined a system that helps organizations not only function but also flourish.

P.E.E.R. is more than a model. It is a leadership philosophy, one that reminds us that strong programs are never accidents. It is built with intention, guided by process, and powered by people who show up with purpose.

As you step into the following chapters, you will discover how to apply P.E.E.R. to your own work, your team, and your mission. Whether you are leading a business, a nonprofit, a small business, or any effort that requires people to work together toward a shared goal, this framework will give you the tools you need to build systems that last.

And like every meaningful system, it begins with a simple decision: to grow on purpose.

PART I: PLAN

"Plan" is the disciplined process of defining purpose, priorities, and measurable goals that guide all future decision

Vision

If you have ever tried to lead a program without a clear vision, you know it is like driving a car with a blindfold on a straight highway. You can move forward, but eventually you will run off the road. The problem is not the car's systems, design, tires, or steering. The problem is quite literally a lack of vision. Similarly, if you try to drive from Texas to New Jersey without any directional support or planning, you may get there eventually, but not as quickly or efficiently as if you had planned the trip and put the right systems in place to get clear directions.

Robert stopped in front of the old metal-and-brick warehouse with bright yellow doors, ready for his first day as the program manager for a local non-profit. He was wearing a pair of faded blue jeans and a grey hoodie, well-kept but intentionally dressed down to ensure he could relate to the population he was serving. During the interview, the founder told him that we cater to San Antonio's lowest-income population "in many ways." That was it, no other clarifying information, usually this would have been a red flag for Robert, but times were tough, and he had already been out of work for four months; he needed this job; his savings needed this job.

When Robert attended his first weekly huddle, he quickly realized the team did not lack enthusiasm; they lacked direction. Everyone had their own version of the program's purpose, ranging from "provide services to the community" (helpful but vague) to "fix the entire city" (ambitious, also vague) to "I don't know, I just work here" (alarmingly honest). Robert knew this showed signs of a program without a vision: well-meaning people rowing in opposite directions, wondering why the boat isn't moving.

Vision provides the force that will keep the team, company, or program in motion. Jim Collins famously wrote that greatness is not a function of circumstance but of conscious choice. In program management, a vision statement is that choice. It is the decision to stop drifting and start aiming.

The problem is that many leaders assume they "sort of know" the vision. But "sort of knowing" is the organizational equivalent of eyeballing measurements when building a structure that must support weight. It might look fine at first, but eventually something collapses.

Teams without a clear vision communicate less effectively, experience higher conflict, and make slower decisions. This step is often sped through and designed by a Google search or ChatGPT prompt without any thought of whether it allows proper alignment with

Robert made the same mistake. In his second week, he created the vision statement "Help people help others." While this may be a good motto or slogan, it is a horrible mission statement. It showed he did not understand the vision, and he hoped clarity would magically appear if he gave it a name. It did not.

The realization hit during a meeting where three staff members described the program using three entirely different metaphors. One said they were "building a ship." Another believed they were "planting a garden." A third insisted the program felt like "juggling chainsaws blindfolded." The problem was not creativity. It was that no one shared a definition of success. A vision statement solves that.

A good vision statement does three things:

- A good vision statement will state the destination clearly.
- A good vision statement will explain why the destination matters.
- A good vision statement will give people a guide for decision-making.

The challenge is writing it in plain language. Many organizations create vision statements so vague that they could describe anything from a nonprofit to a scented candle brand. Others make statements so poetic that no one can remember them without reading the website. As Patrick Lencioni once joked, most vision statements sound like they were written by committee because they were.

Robert learned quickly that clarity beats cleverness. His first attempt at a vision statement was forty-five words long and used the phrase "holistic synergy" twice. After deleting it, he tried again, and by the seventh attempt, he was not writing a vision statement; he was drafting an essay.

The final breakthrough came when he stopped asking, "What should this sound like?" and instead asked, "What problem does this program actually exist to solve, and what would success look like if we solved it well?"

That question changed everything.

He returned the next day with a single sentence. It was not flashy or poetic, but everyone understood it immediately. More importantly, everyone agreed. And agreement is the first sign that a vision is working.

Application: How Robert Applied Vision in Practice

Robert did not apply vision by printing it on a poster or tucking it into the footer of a slide deck. He applied how vision functions in real programs: as a reference that can govern decisions when pressure rises, and clarity is assessed.

When Robert first stepped into leadership, the absence of a shared vision made everything feel rushed and busy. Meetings were happening, staff were active, and progress looked good on paper. This is precisely what the Project Management Institute warns about: misalignment with defined outcomes, leading to inefficiency disguised as productivity [12].

Treating Vision Like a Program Charter

PMI defines a charter as the mechanism that authorizes work and serves as a reference point for decision-making among stakeholders [12]. Robert realized his program had activity but no shared authorization logic. People were not making poor decisions; they were making *different* decisions based on various assumptions.

He reduced the vision to a single sentence that clearly stated who the program served, what outcome defined success, and what work fell outside the program's purpose. PMI notes that clarity of intent significantly reduces scope creep and stakeholder conflict later in execution [12]. If the vision required explanation, it was not ready.

Pressure-Testing Vision Against Real Decisions

Robert did not announce the vision in a meeting. He tested it in practice. Every proposal passed through one filter: "Does this move us closer to the vision, or does it simply keep us busy?"

When a long-standing initiative failed that test, Robert asked the team to explain how it aligned. When no one could, the decision became clear. This reflects Jim Collins's principle of disciplined decision-making, where successful organizations choose *not* to do in the service of a clear direction [13].

Once vision became non-negotiable, decision-making accelerated, and productivity increased.

Embedding Vision into Daily Operations

Vision only works when people choose to use and respect it. Robert embedded vision into hiring conversations, budget decisions, and weekly planning meetings. PMI's benefits-realization research emphasizes that programs succeed when strategy development is connected to execution, not revisited only during planning cycles [14].

Using Vision to Reduce Conflict

Vision did not eliminate disagreement; it reframed it. Patrick Lencioni notes that healthy organizations argue productively because they are aligned on purpose, not because they avoid tension [15]. Robert began redirecting discussions back to the vision, which allowed decisions to be structural rather than emotional.

Revisiting Vision as Conditions Changed

Robert also learned that vision is not static. PMI emphasizes adaptability as a core leadership responsibility when external conditions shift [12]. When the community's needs evolved, Robert reviewed and refined the vision without defensiveness. Vision was not a sacred text; it was a living reference point.

Blueprint for the Reader

Robert's approach can be replicated:

1. Write vision as a decision-making sentence.
2. Use it as a filter before approving work, not after problems arise.
3. Embed it into operations, not orientation materials.
4. Redirect conflict back to purpose, not personalities.
5. Review vision when reality changes, not when morale drops.

Problem identification

Trying to build, run, or manage a program without first identifying the problem you are trying to solve is like treating an illness without evaluating its symptoms. You can keep handing out medications, but if the real issue is a compound fracture, nothing gets better. Programs collapse for the same reason: leaders throw solutions at the problem without first clearly identifying it. This lack of clarity can lead to overworked employees and redundant systems.

Robert wanted to know precisely what the organization was trying to do for the community; what problems they were trying to solve. So, in his second weekly huddle, he asked his team what they thought the problem was. Their eyes darted, hoping frantically that someone knew. One person confidently explains the problem, only to reveal they have absolutely no idea what is going on. And at least one person decided now is the perfect time to refill their coffee.

This is not because people are incompetent; it is because most programs begin with enthusiasm rather than diagnosis. Robert saw this when he inherited an initiative that looked like a collection of ideas that were never tied to a central goal or mission statement. The previous manager left behind 47 documents, none of which agreed with the others. One file said the program existed to improve literacy rates. Another said its purpose was community wellness. A third document ambitiously declared the program's mission was to "restore harmony to the human condition," which Robert suspected was either a joke or a misfiled philosophy paper. Nobody had identified the problem they were setting out to solve.

A program without a defined problem statement is like attempting to assemble furniture without instructions and deciding the finished product is "whatever happens." You end up with a wobbly structure, a spare bag of screws, and an unsettling feeling that something vital is upside down.

Research backs this up. Studies in organizational effectiveness show that incorrect problem identification is the single largest cause of strategic failure [1]. Teams invest time, money, and emotional energy into solving problems that are not problems, at least not the right ones. Robert's team had precisely done this. They were attempting to fix symptoms, not causes. The result was predictable: exhaustion with no progress. To break the cycle, Robert needed to identify the real problem.

This required what Robert called Organizational Archeology, digging through layers of paperwork, interviewing staff who had been around long enough to remember when the program's logo still had clip art, and asking the right questions like:

"Why do we have this meeting every Thursday?"

"Who requested this?"

"Has anyone checked if this is working since 2014?"

The answers were revealing.

One staff member responded, "We typically do Thursday meetings because we've always done Thursday activities," which clarified absolutely nothing. Another admitted they were not sure who the program was meant to help, only that "people show up sometimes, typically for help with food or other resources," which was accurate but not helpful. A third person confessed they did not know the problem, which Robert recognized as the universal anthem of dysfunctional organizations. Each of these statements was either preceded by or followed by the word typically, which is progressions' kryptonite.

Eventually, patterns emerged, indicating that the program was not failing due to a lack of effort. It was failing because no one had named the real issue: the community's needs had changed, but the program had not kept pace. That was the problem, not funding or not staffing. The real issue was misalignment between what the community needed and what the program was doing.

This realization was both humbling and relieving. It meant the team was not trying to fix the wrong things; they were all trying to fix everything. As Harvard Business Review notes, "Organizations struggle most when their solutions outlive the problems they were created to address" [2]. Robert's program was a perfect example: it was built for a community that no longer existed.

Robert realized the only way to move forward was to articulate the problem statement in a single, brutally honest sentence.

Not a paragraph.

Not a manifesto.

Not motivational speech.

Just one sentence that accurately captured what they were up against.

This took courage because clarity often does. A clear problem statement eliminates excuses. It removes convenient ambiguity. At one end of the spectrum, it forces everyone to face reality, not the version of reality they wish were true; on the other, it empowers the team. Once a problem is identified, they can work together. Robert drafted several versions before landing on a statement that made everyone nod, sigh, or suddenly sit up straighter.

He did not aim for elegance; he aimed for accuracy.

And the moment the team accepted the real problem, the program finally had a starting point. No matter how well-designed a program is, every goal, every resource, every decision must be traced back to solving the right problem; If it does not, it will not be successful.

Application: How Robert Applied Core Problem Identification in Practice

Robert did not realize how dangerous a poorly defined problem could be until he watched an entire team work themselves into exhaustion while technically doing everything "right." Tasks were completed. Meetings were held. Reports were written. And yet, progress had stalled. That experience forced him to confront a truth most leaders avoid: solving the wrong problem efficiently is still failure.

The Project Management Institute notes that one of the most common causes of program underperformance is misalignment between perceived problems and actual root causes, especially in complex environments where urgency overrides analysis [1]. Robert saw this firsthand. Every time something went wrong, the team reacted quickly, but never collectively. Funding was blamed for one week. Staffing next week. Engagement after that. Each response made sense in isolation, but none addressed the underlying issue.

Treating Problem Identification as a Leadership Responsibility

Harvard Business Review highlights that organizations often fail not because problems are hidden, but because leaders mislabel symptoms as causes and rush to action without diagnosis [2]. Robert recognized himself in that description. He had been managing noise, not root causes.

So, he slowed the program down briefly and intentionally. This was not popular. People equate speed with competence. But Robert understood that clarity precedes momentum, not the other way around.

He began by separating symptoms from causes. Low participation was a symptom. Staff burnout was a symptom. Delayed outcomes were a symptom. The real question was "what those symptoms revealed when combined."

Digging for the Root Cause

Robert approached problem identification the way a project manager approaches risk analysis: methodically. PMI emphasizes that effective leaders distinguish between surface-level issues and systemic drivers before allocating resources [12]. Robert reviewed historical documents, interviewed long-term staff, and examined original assumptions baked into the program years earlier.

What emerged was uncomfortable but clear. The program was still structured around a population and a need that no longer existed. Community dynamics had shifted. Expectations had changed. The program had not.

This matched what Harvard Business Review describes as "solution inertia," in which organizations continue to execute outdated solutions long after the problem has evolved [2]. Robert realized the team was not underperforming; they were misaligned.

Reducing the Problem to One Sentence

The most challenging part was articulation. Robert resisted the urge to write a paragraph. PMI guidance emphasizes that clarity improves execution only when it is concise enough to guide decisions consistently [12].

He wrote the core problem in a single sentence, limiting distractions from the intent. The statement did not blame people; it described reality. When he shared it, something shifted, and people finally looked relieved. Misalignment created tension; clarity released it.

Using the Core Problem as a Decision Filter

Once the problem was identified, Robert stopped asking whether ideas were "good" and started asking whether they addressed the core problem. This mirrors Jim Collins's concept of disciplined focus—where progress comes from consistent alignment rather than scattered excellence [13].

Projects that did not address the problem were paused or eliminated. This was not popular at first, but it was effective. Meetings shortened. Priorities clarified. Energy returned.

The Project Management Institute's research on global program trends emphasizes that successful programs allocate resources based on strategic relevance rather than historical habit [1]. Robert finally had a defensible way to do that precisely.

Aligning People Around the Problem

Problem clarity also changed how people worked together. Instead of debating preferences, the team debated approaches. Patrick Lencioni notes that healthy teams argue productively when they are aligned on purpose [15]. Robert stopped mediating the conflict and began referring to the problem statement. It became the neutral third party in every discussion.

People stopped protecting their ideas and started protecting alignment.

Revisiting the Problem Over Time

Robert also learned that core problems are not permanent. PMI emphasizes adaptability as a leadership requirement in dynamic environments [12]. He scheduled periodic reviews of the problem statement to anticipate any changes in the environment in which the organization operated. This prevented the program from reverting to assumption-driven decision-making.

Blueprint for the Reader

Robert's approach can be replicated:

1. Slow down long enough to diagnose before acting.
2. Write the core problem as one concise sentence.
3. Use it as a reference for priorities and resources.
4. Revise or replace it as conditions change.

Organizations do not fail because they lack effort; they fail because they do not focus on the right problem. As Harvard Business Review notes, early misidentification of problems compounds over time, turning manageable issues into systemic failures [2].

Target Population

Identifying your target population is the professional version of knowing who you are cooking for. You can prepare the world's best lasagna, but if your guests are gluten-intolerant and allergic to tomatoes, you have missed the mark entirely. Programs fail for the same reason: they are built for the wrong audience.

In his third week, Robert proudly unveiled a new outreach plan only to discover that it appealed to a demographic that did not exist anywhere within a 30-mile radius. It was the organizational equivalent of designing a senior water aerobics program for a town where the average resident was twenty-nine—a bold idea, just wildly unhelpful.

Research consistently shows that programs tightly aligned with clearly defined populations outperform general initiatives by significant margins [1]. The problem is that many leaders skip this step entirely because it feels limiting, when determining your population is what sets you free. You cannot help everyone, but you can make a meaningful impact if you know exactly who you are trying to serve.

Robert approached this realization with a method I call "Demographic Reality Check," which is a polite way of saying he finally stopped guessing. He reviewed community data, interviewed stakeholders, examined past attendance patterns, and, most importantly, asked the question leaders regularly avoid: "Who is this program actually for?"

The answers revealed that the program had been unintentionally targeting three incompatible groups simultaneously: retirees, single parents, and teenagers. This explained why scheduling was impossible, communication was chaotic, and events felt like three different committee meetings happening inside the same room. No program can survive being pulled in that many directions.

Once Robert clarified the actual target population in this case, working-age adults seeking practical skill development, everything changed. Program hours shifted. Messaging shifted. Activities shifted.

And for the first time, participation began to increase. The magic was in proper alignment between the demographics and the services.

A clearly defined population sharpens every decision, from communication style to staffing to resource allocation. It prevents scope creep, burnout, and "Frankenprograms," stitched together from the remains of well-intentioned ideas that no longer fit the mission. Most importantly, it allows the program to serve real humans instead of a vague concept of "the community," which is organizational code for "we don't actually know who we're helping."

Robert's breakthrough was not discovering new techniques; it was finding who the program existed for. Once he understood that, everything else began to fall into place.

Application: How Robert Applied the Target Population in Practice

Like many leaders, Robert had worked in many jobs serving a target population before his hiring, so he never had to think much about it. Early on, he thought serving "the community" sounded inclusive and noble. In practice, it was paralyzing.

The first sign that something was wrong was not attendance; it was inconsistency. Some events were full. Others were empty. Messaging reached a few people but completely missed others. Scheduling debates became endless. Robert realized that some programs were failing because they were unfocused.

PMI's research on global program trends emphasizes that initiatives aligned to clearly defined beneficiaries consistently outperform those designed for broad or ambiguous audiences [1]. Robert was doing the opposite. He was trying to create a single program for multiple, incompatible populations and hoping that the effort would close the gap.

Moving from Assumption to Evidence

Robert's first mistake was assuming that past attendance equaled relevance. Harvard Business Review points out that organizations often mistake historical participation for current need, failing to reassess who their solutions truly serve as conditions change [2]. Robert had been building for yesterday's audience.

He began collecting data, reviewing attendance patterns, intake forms, referral sources, and completion rates. He spoke directly with participants and, more importantly, with people who stopped coming. This shift mirrored PMI's guidance that stakeholder analysis must be revisited throughout a program lifecycle, not assumed at launch [12].

What he discovered was that the program was unintentionally attracting three separate groups with competing needs. No schedule, message, or activity could serve all three well. The program was not underperforming; it was overextended.

Defining the Population Narrowly—on Purpose

Once Robert accepted that specificity creates impact, not exclusion, progress accelerated. Research on organizational effectiveness shows that focus improves outcomes by enabling leaders to tailor goals, resources, and communication [3]. Robert selected one primary population based on the severity of need, readiness to engage, and alignment with program capabilities.

What Robert learned matched findings from social innovation research: programs that define beneficiaries narrowly deliver more profound, more sustainable impact than those that attempt to serve everyone simultaneously [4].

Aligning Goals to the Population

With the population defined, Robert rewrote the goals. Locke and Latham's goal-setting research emphasizes that goals are most effective when they are specific and directly tied to the people performing and benefiting from the work [3]. Generic goals disappeared. Measurable, population-specific goals took their place.

Instead of "increase engagement," goals became "increase consistent participation among working-age adults over a six-week cycle." This level of precision changed how success was measured and discussed.

Rebuilding Communication Around the Audience

Target population clarity transformed communication. Robert stopped sending one-size-fits-all messages and began tailoring language, channels, and cadence to how the population consumed information. Research on multi-channel communication confirms that engagement increases when communication methods align with audience behavior rather than organizational convenience [8].

The result was shorter emails, more pointed digital feedback programs, and messaging shifted from promotional to practical. Participation stabilized almost immediately.

Adjusting Partnerships and Resources

Defining the population also clarified partnerships. Robert stopped pursuing collaborations that looked impressive but did not serve the chosen audience. Stanford Social Innovation Review notes that cross-sector partnerships are most effective when built around shared beneficiaries rather than shared branding [4]. Robert focused on partners already trusted by the target population, which increased credibility and referrals.

Resources followed clarity. Time, staff energy, and materials were allocated based on actual needs instead of assumptions. PMI emphasizes that benefits realization depends on aligning resources to stakeholder value, not organizational habit [1]. Robert finally had a defensible way to do that.

Using Feedback to Validate the Population Choice

Feedback confirmed the shift. The Organizational Behavior Institute highlights that feedback systems reveal whether alignment decisions are working in practice [5]. Participants reported clearer expectations. Staff reported reduced confusion; outcomes became predictable rather than erratic. Robert also noticed who *was no longer showing up*. Some disengagement was expected. Targeting is not rejection; it is alignment.

Blueprint for the Reader

Robert's approach can be replicated:

1. Define one primary population intentionally.
2. Align goals directly to that population's needs [3]
3. Tailor communication methods to audience behavior [8]
4. Choose partners based on shared beneficiaries, not convenience [4]
5. Use feedback to validate and refine alignment [5]

Programs fail when they try to serve everyone well. They succeed when they serve the right people exceptionally well. As PMI's global research makes clear, clarity about who benefits is a prerequisite for sustainable impact [1]. Robert did not limit his program by defining the target population. He unlocked it.

Partners

Identifying key partners is not about forming alliances for the sake of looking collaborative; it is about strategically aligning with the people and organizations who fill the gaps your program cannot fill alone.

Robert realized that a volunteer staff often viewed the program as optional rather than a priority. When the care seekers drastically outnumbered the caregivers in his organization, Robert learned the importance of building relationships with individuals and organizations who could assist with the mission, even if they were not listed on the program's organizational chart.

According to strategic partnership research, programs that intentionally build cross-functional relationships experience 30–50% higher operational stability [1]. That is because partners provide critical access to resources, expertise, and networks that programs cannot generate internally. Robert started mapping out every individual or group whose actions influenced the outcomes of his program. The list was longer than he expected: facilities, IT support, the finance office, communications staff, external nonprofits, local schools, and, unexpectedly, the city librarian, who turned out to be more connected than a Fortune 500 CEO.

The more Robert networked, the clearer it became that programs function as ecosystems, not silos. The success of one component inevitably depends on the reliability of others. Ignoring this reality is a fast track to frustration, miscommunication, and the type of problem leaders optimistically describe as 'unexpected,' even though everyone knew it was going to happen.

Once Robert identified his key partners, the next step was establishing clarity. Partners cannot support your program if they do not understand two things: what you need and why it matters. Robert scheduled brief, informal relationship-building meetings (which he referred to privately as 'diplomatic reconnaissance'). This simple step brought two unexpected benefits: first, partners felt appreciated; second, they began offering support proactively.

The most successful programs treat their key partners like customers. Holding communication in high regard and expressing gratitude regularly. Studies on organizational collaboration show that positive relational equity, people feeling valued within a partnership, increases cooperation by up to 70% [2]. Robert saw this firsthand when the previously elusive IT department suddenly began responding to requests within hours rather than days.

Partnerships are not just functional; they are strategic. They multiply a program's capacity, expertise, and credibility. Without alliances, leaders end up spending most of their time working on things that do not align with their mission. With strong and clear partnerships, leaders can focus on solving meaningful problems rather than surviving logistical disasters.

Robert did not need more staff; he needed better alignment. And once he found the right partners, the program no longer wanted to push a weighted sled uphill; it felt coordinated, supported, and much more manageable.

Application: How Robert Applied Strategic Partnerships in Practice

Robert used to think partnerships were about goodwill and proximity. If an organization was nearby, well-known, or friendly, it felt logical to call them a partner. That assumption did not last long. The first time a critical dependency failed, Robert realized: partnerships are not relationships you collect; they are systems you design.

PMI's research on program performance highlights that outcomes improve when leaders intentionally identify and manage stakeholders who directly influence delivery, rather than relying on informal cooperation [1]. Robert had plenty of friendly contacts but very few *operationally aligned* partners.

Instead of asking, *"Who supports our mission?"* Robert asked, "Who directly affects our ability to deliver outcomes, whether they realize it or not?"

Mapping the Real Partnership Ecosystem

Robert used a mapping exercise. He listed every individual, team, and organization whose actions could delay, disrupt, or strengthen the program. The list was longer than expected. It included facilities, IT, finance, communications, external nonprofits, referral sources, and municipal departments. Some did not think of themselves as partners at all.

This approach aligns with PMI's guidance that stakeholder influence extends beyond formal agreements and must be identified early to reduce risk and misalignment [12]. Robert was not building alliances for optics; he was designing reliability into the system.

Shifting from Courtesy to Clarity

In early conversations, Robert discovered that many "partners" did not understand the program, its priorities, or why their role mattered. Stanford Social Innovation Review emphasizes that cross-sector partnerships fail most often due to unclear expectations and misaligned incentives, rather than a lack of trust [4]. Robert had assumed shared values would equal shared understanding. They did not.

He corrected this by clarifying three things in every partnership conversation:

- What the program needs
- Why it Mattered
- Which partner best fills that need?

These conversations were brief but intentional. Robert did not over-formalize them, but he documented agreements and dependencies. Fluff-filled ideology was replaced with concise clarity, which reduced friction.

Aligning Partnerships to the Target Population

Defining the target population sharpened partnership decisions. Robert stopped pursuing relationships that looked impressive but did not serve the program's purpose. Stanford Social Innovation Review notes that partnerships deliver impact when they are built around shared beneficiaries rather than shared branding [4]. This insight has been shown to save time, increase credibility, and improve resource utilization.

He prioritized partners already trusted by the population, organizations that participants recognized and relied on. Referrals improved. Attendance stabilized. The program's reputation strengthened without additional marketing.

Treating Partners as Operational Stakeholders

Robert also changed how he communicated. Instead of reaching out only when something was needed, he built a routine of updates and check-ins, some of which were nothing more than a 5-minute phone call focused solely on building a relationship. Learning & Development Quarterly highlights that consistent, multi-channel communication strengthens collaboration by reducing assumptions and delays [8]. Robert applied that principle to partnerships.

Short updates replaced long explanations. Advance notice replaced last-minute requests. Partners felt informed rather than used. Response times improved dramatically, not because Robert demanded urgency, but because partners understood relevance.

Managing Risk Through Partnership Design

Robert learned that partnerships are also a form of risk control. PMI emphasizes that effective programs mitigate risk by identifying dependencies and building redundancy where possible [12]. When one partner was unavailable, Robert ensured another could fill the gap. No single organization held the program hostage if they had competing obligations. This mindset shifted partnerships from reactive problem-solving to proactive stability. Risks became manageable instead of disruptive.

Measuring Partnership Effectiveness

Robert did not assume partnerships were working; he evaluated them. The Organizational Behavior Institute notes that feedback systems improve team performance when applied consistently across relationships [5]. Robert asked partners for feedback and paid attention to delays, miscommunications, and bottlenecks. Partnerships that created more friction than value were redesigned or released. This was not personal. It was strategic.

Blueprint for the Reader

Robert's approach can be replicated:

1. Map all stakeholders who influence delivery, not just formal partners [12]
2. Clarify expectations, dependencies, and success measures early [4]

3. Align partnerships to the defined target population, not prestige [4]
4. Communicate consistently using clear, appropriate channels [8]
5. Design partnerships as risk mitigators, not conveniences [12]
6. Evaluate partnerships using feedback and performance indicators [5]

Programs do not operate in isolation; they operate in ecosystems. As PMI's global research shows, leaders who intentionally manage those ecosystems achieve stronger outcomes and greater stability [1]. Robert did not add more partners to fix his program. He built the *right* partnerships, and the program finally stopped feeling fragile.

Resources

In program management, resources fall into four predictable categories: people, time, money, and tools. All four are necessary and are often in short supply. Leaders usually try to compensate for missing resources by overworking themselves, which is admirable but unsustainable and, according to most studies on workforce performance, wildly ineffective [1]. Programs thrive not because leaders hustle harder but because leaders allocate smarter.

Robert's first attempt at resource planning involved listing everything he wished he had: laptops, dedicated staff, transportation vouchers, marketing materials, training budgets, reliable Wi-Fi, and most critically, coffee that did not taste like budget despair. But wish lists do not create functional programs; prioritization does.

Robert lived by the rule that resource planning began with identifying what is essential versus what is helpful. Essentials are anything that directly impacts program delivery. Helpful resources were those that improved quality but would not cause the program to collapse if temporarily missing. This distinction alone saved him from dozens of unnecessary purchases and several emotional breakdowns.

When he first began his career, he did his best to avoid scarcity but discovered that scarcity often forces innovation. When Robert realized he could not afford new laptops for his team, he partnered with a local tech nonprofit to refurbish donated ones. This decision saved thousands of dollars and unexpectedly upgraded the program's public image. Research shows that constraints can increase creativity and improve problem-solving by focusing attention on what truly matters [2]. Scarcity is not always the enemy; sometimes, it is a catalyst.

Human resources, not the department, but actual humans. People are the most valuable and least predictable resource in any program. Volunteers, staff, contractors, and community partners all bring different skills, motivations, and limitations. Robert learned that assigning tasks based purely on availability was a mistake. Effective programs match people's strengths to program needs; a practice linked to higher satisfaction and performance [3].

Finally, Robert recognized that time is the most misunderstood resource. Leaders treat time as flexible until it suddenly is not. Programs do not fail because people run out of hours; they fail because they misuse the hours they have. Robert created a simple time budget that mapped out weekly demands and revealed a shocking truth: the program required 50 hours of staff labor per week, yet only twenty-eight were available. No amount of optimism can bend time. Adjustments had to be made. Robert found that streamlining systems, reducing redundancy, and making slight modifications to duty descriptions saved time and dramatically reduced burnout.

By the end of his resource analysis, Robert no longer saw resources as limitations. He saw them as variables to manage. Some he could expand, some he could borrow, and some he could creatively replace. But all of them mattered. Programs that ignore resource requirements do not become inspirational success stories; they become case studies in preventable failure.

Robert's transformation was not dramatic. It was practical. He stopped wishing for more resources and started maximizing the ones he had. And in program management, that shift makes all the difference.

Application: How Robert Applied Resource Management in Practice

Robert learned very quickly that resource problems rarely announce themselves as "resource problems." They show up disguised as exhaustion, missed deadlines, frustrated staff, and the quiet realization that everyone is doing their best and still falling behind. Early on, he believed what many leaders believed: if people cared enough, they would find a way to make things work. What he learned instead was that caring without structure burns people out faster.

The Project Management Institute notes that one of the most consistent predictors of program underperformance is poor alignment between available resources and actual workload demands [1]. Robert did not need a report to confirm this. He watched capable people juggle too much responsibility while critical tasks slipped through the cracks.

Treating Resources as Variables, Not Obstacles

Robert's first mistake was treating resources as fixed limitations. If funding was low, he accepted stress as inevitable. If staffing was thin, he normalized overwork. But research shows that programs that intentionally assess and rebalance resources outperform those that rely on improvisation and goodwill [1]. Robert realized that resources are variables to be managed, not excuses to be endured.

He began by listing all four core resource categories: people, time, money, and tools. Then he mapped them against actual program requirements. He found that the program required more hours than existed, more skills than were available, and more tools than were funded. Thankfully, it was not too late for change. Robert and his team got to work, listing and realigning the available resources to ensure the program ran smoothly.

Reallocating Instead of Overworking

Rather than demanding more effort, Robert reduced the scope. He eliminated tasks that did not directly support program goals. Harvard Business Review highlights that organizations often exhaust resources by continuing legacy activities long after they stop adding value [2]. Robert recognized several such activities immediately. They were familiar, visible, and ineffective. Cutting them saved time without costing morale. Staff did not feel punished; they felt relieved.

Using Scarcity to Drive Focus

Scarcity forced prioritization. Instead of spreading resources thin, Robert concentrated them where impact was highest. Research on incremental improvement shows that minor, focused adjustments outperform sweeping reforms because they are easier to implement and sustain [10]. Robert adopted this mindset. He did not try to fix everything at once. He made one meaningful resource adjustment per cycle.

When funding was limited, he sought partnerships to supplement tools and space. When staffing was thin, he simplified workflows. When time was constrained, he redesigned schedules rather than extending them. Scarcity stopped being the enemy; it became the filter.

Matching People to Strengths

Robert realized that people are not interchangeable resources. Assigning tasks based on availability created inefficiency and frustration. Research on goal setting and task alignment shows that performance improves when responsibilities align with individual strengths and when the clarity of purpose is high [3]. Robert reassigned tasks based on capability, not convenience. This reduced mistakes, increased ownership, and improved morale almost immediately. People did not work harder; they worked better.

Making Time Visible

Time was the most mismanaged resource. Robert assumed time was flexible until it was not. He tracked how long tasks took and discovered that expectations were consistently unrealistic. Robert knew from past lessons that programs do not suffer because people waste time; it is because leaders underestimate it.

Once time management became a priority, decisions improved, deadlines became achievable, and meetings shortened. Most importantly, the program stopped operating in a constant state of urgency. PMI emphasizes that realistic scheduling and workload awareness are essential to sustainable performance [12], and Robert finally understood why.

Protecting Resources Through Structure

Robert also built guardrails. He implemented simple approval rules, workload caps, and decision filters to prevent resources from being drained by urgency alone. Research on workplace efficiency shows that unmanaged barriers and interruptions significantly reduce productivity [7]. By reducing friction, Robert preserved capacity without adding cost.

Blueprint for the Reader

Robert's approach can be replicated:

1. Inventory people, time, money, and tools honestly.
2. Compare resources to actual workload.
3. Eliminate activities that do not add value [2]
4. Use scarcity as a focus mechanism [10]
5. Match tasks to strengths, not availability [3]
6. Make time visible and protect it with structure [12]
7. Reduce friction to preserve capacity [7]

Risks & Mitigation

Every program looks brilliant on a whiteboard. It is only when the real world enters the chat that everything gets interesting. Risks are not signs of poor planning, incompetence, or bad leadership; failing to recognize and mitigate them is, though. Robert learned this during his first official program audit, when he proudly walked in expecting to highlight his progress and instead walked out holding a list of twenty-seven risks the inspectors found in his program.

Program risks fall into four predictable buckets: operational, financial, personnel-related, and external. Ignoring risks does not make them disappear; it makes them stronger. Research from the Project Management Institute shows that programs with formal risk-identification processes are 38% more likely to succeed than those that rely on optimism as a strategy [1].

Robert knew it was a mistake to assume risks were always dramatic events like fires, lawsuits, rogue employees forming underground committees. Most often, risks are much subtler and include missed deadlines, unclear communication, insufficient staffing, outdated equipment, and processes that rely on a single employee. These are the risks that drain time, destroy morale, and turn good programs into chaos.

Robert knew from experience that if something could go wrong, he should assume it would. This was not pessimism, but it was preparation. Instead of panicking when a staff member quit suddenly, he began developing cross-training plans. Instead of scrambling when funding fluctuated, he created budget tiers. Instead of praying the printer would cooperate, he finally negotiated access to two backup machines in other departments.

Mitigation, Robert discovered, is not about preventing problems entirely. The primary purpose is to reduce the level of chaos upon their arrival. A good mitigation plan answers three questions:

1. What could realistically go wrong?

2. What would we do if it happened?

3. How do we make sure we are not surprised by this again?

Operational risks were the easiest to identify, including issues with schedules, supplies, workload, or workflow. Robert mapped these by walking through a typical program day and documenting all the places where something could break. Financial risks required honesty about the budget, grant deadlines, and the ever-popular 'imaginary funding' line items beloved by overly optimistic directors.

Personnel-related risks were more delicate. People bring strengths, but they also bring limitations, stress, burnout, and the occasional dramatic resignation email written entirely in capital letters. Robert learned to identify risks related to skill gaps, bottleneck roles, and communication styles that produced more confusion than clarity. This helped him redesign responsibilities to prevent individual burnout and dangerous dependence on a single employee.

External risks included shifting community needs, partner organizations changing direction, technology updates, and policy changes that arrived with no warning and with the subtlety of a marching band. These were not controllable, but they were predictable enough to plan around.

By the time Robert completed his first formal risk assessment, he discovered something surprising: risks were not threats; they were guideposts. Each one showed him where the program needed reinforcement and provided clear direction for improvement. Once corrected, risk mitigation transformed uncertainty into a strategy.

Programs that plan for risks do not avoid challenges; they navigate them with significantly less panic. And in program management, reduced panic counts as measurable progress.

Application: How Robert Applied Risk Management and Mitigation in Practice

Robert did not think of himself as someone who ignored risk. In fact, he believed he was cautious. What he eventually learned, however, was that caution without structure is doomed to fail. Risks were always present in the program; he just had not named, tracked, or prepared for them in a way that made them manageable.

The Project Management Institute consistently identifies unmanaged risk as one of the primary reasons programs miss objectives, overrun budgets, or lose stakeholder confidence [1]. Robert experienced this firsthand. Problems kept appearing "unexpectedly," yet when he looked back, none of them were surprises. They were patterns he had not documented.

Reframing Risk as Operational Reality

Robert's first breakthrough was recognizing that most risks are not dramatic. They do not arrive with sirens or warning emails. They show up as missed handoffs, unclear responsibilities, inconsistent communication, and quiet dependency on one person. Harvard Business Review notes that organizations often fail to identify risks early because they normalize small failures, which can compound [2].

He categorized risks into four practical groups: operational, financial, personnel, and external. This simple structure allowed the team to talk about risk without panic. Naming risks did not make the program feel fragile; it made it feel honest.

Identifying Risks Through Process Walkthroughs

Rather than brainstorming hypotheticals, Robert walked through the program step by step. Every activity was examined for failure points. Where could communication break down? Where was a task dependent on a single person? Where did timing assumptions exceed reality?

This approach mirrors PMI guidance that effective risk identification is grounded in process analysis rather than speculation [12]. Robert documented risks in plain language—no jargon or scoring models at first. The result was clarity: risks that had felt overwhelming became visible, reducing fear.

Prioritizing Risks Instead of Fixing Everything

Robert made another critical mistake early on: trying to mitigate every risk at once. It did not work. Research on incremental improvement confirms that attempting large-scale fixes simultaneously often creates resistance and fatigue [10]. Robert adjusted his approach.

He prioritized risks based on two criteria:

- Likelihood of occurrence
- Impact on program outcomes

Only high-likelihood, high-impact risks were addressed immediately. Others were monitored. This prevented the team from being overwhelmed by mitigation plans and made progress feel achievable.

Building Mitigation into Daily Operations

Mitigation stopped being a separate activity and became part of how the program ran. If a role created a risk due to single-person dependency, Robert cross-trained someone else. To address funding volatility, he created tiered budgets. If communication delays were frequent, he clarified channels and response expectations.

Research on workplace efficiency shows that reducing everyday barriers has a greater impact on stability than reacting to major failures [7]. Robert focused on friction reduction rather than perfection.

Preparing for External Risks Without Obsession

Not all risks were controllable. Policy changes, partner availability, technology failures, and community shifts fell outside Robert's direct influence. PMI emphasizes that leaders cannot eliminate external risks, but they can plan responses that reduce disruption [12]. Robert documented "if–then" responses:

- If a partner becomes unavailable, then an alternate is activated.
- If attendance drops, then outreach methods adjust.
- If funding decreases, then the scope reduces rather than the workloads increasing.

This preparation prevented panic. When disruptions occurred, the team executed rather than reacted.

Using Communication to Strengthen Mitigation

Communication played a leading role in risk mitigation. Having Learning & Development Meetings that highlight multi-channel communication reduces the likelihood of errors during high-stress situations [8]. Robert ensured that critical risk responses were communicated clearly, repeatedly, and across multiple channels. Staff knew who decided what. Volunteers knew who to contact. Confusion decreased, and, with it, risk was effectively mitigated.

Creating a Risk-Aware Culture

The most important shift was culture. Robert stopped treating risk identification as a form of criticism. Staff were encouraged to report vulnerabilities early. This aligns with organizational research showing that feedback-rich environments surface risks before they escalate [5]. Risk discussions became standard practice, resulting in much less day-to-day chaos.

Blueprint for the Reader

Robert's approach can be replicated:

1. Reframe risk as operational reality.
2. Identify risks by walking real processes [12]
3. Categorize risks to reduce emotional response.
4. Prioritize based on likelihood and impact.
5. Mitigate through small structural changes [10]
6. Prepare responses for external risks rather than ignoring them.
7. Build a culture where naming risk is encouraged [5]

Timeline

Timelines are where ambition meets reality. They are also where Robert learned that optimism is not a scheduling strategy. In program management, a timeline is less about predicting the future and more about preventing chaos by giving the future a polite warning that you are coming. Without a timeline, every task becomes urgent, every delay becomes a crisis, and every meeting begins with someone asking, "Wait... when was that due?"

Robert's early approach to timelines assumed that everything would take exactly as long as he imagined. This method has historically had a low success rate. His first draft timeline looked like a motivational poster, neatly arranged, beautifully color-coded, and disconnected from reality. By week two, three tasks were overdue, two were forgotten, and one was still listed as 'in progress' despite nobody remembering who was responsible for it.

Programs require timelines because humans require structure. Studies on productivity repeatedly show that tasks without deadlines take exponentially longer to complete [1]. The brain does not prioritize functions without a clear endpoint. Timelines create that endpoint, transforming abstract goals into concrete actions by answering three critical questions:

1. What needs to happen?

2. When does it need to happen?

3. Who is responsible for making it happen?

Robert discovered that timelines are not about speed; they are about sequence. A program may not collapse if something takes longer than expected, but it may collapse if tasks are executed in the wrong order. For example, marketing cannot go out until the program details are available. Staff training cannot occur before staff exist to train. The organization cannot provide grant reports until the budget and mission statements are clearly outlined.

The key to building a functional timeline is reverse engineering to achieve the end goal. Robert began creating timelines by starting with the program launch date and working backward. This process instantly clarified which tasks were essential, which were optional, and which were delusions of grandeur. Reverse engineering also revealed hidden dependencies: small tasks that required five other tasks to occur first.

Another element Robert learned to incorporate was buffer time. Buffer time is the scheduling equivalent of packing an extra pair of socks: you may not need it often, but when you do, it saves you from disaster. Buffer time compensates for unexpected delays, underestimated workloads, and occasional human forgetfulness (which research says is not uncommon [2]). Robert began adding buffer days to every significant milestone and discovered that timelines became attainable rather than aspirational.

Finally, timelines require visibility: A timeline that is not distributed properly and regularly will not be effective. Robert began displaying timelines publicly in staff spaces, sending weekly updates, and conducting short check-ins to ensure everyone knew the upcoming tasks. This not only improved accountability but also reduced the number of people approaching him with panicked expressions asking whether something was supposed to be done 'today or yesterday.'

By the end of his first successful program cycle, Robert learned that timelines are not about perfection. They are about coordination. A reasonable timeline keeps a team aligned; a great timeline keeps a program on track; and an exceptional timeline prevents at least three avoidable emergencies per month. In program management, this slight improvement counts as measurable success.

Application: How Robert Applied Timeline Management in Practice

Robert knew improper timelines were optimistic guesses disguised as plans. He also knew to ensure dates were chosen for their soundness. When deadlines slipped, he adjusted expectations and asked people to "push a little harder." It worked until it did not. Over time, missed dates became normal, urgency replaced planning, and the program operated in a constant state of catch-up.

PMI's research on program performance consistently shows that unrealistic scheduling is a primary contributor to missed objectives and team burnout [1]. Robert did not need a report to tell him that. He could see it in his team's fatigue and the erosion of trust from the partners.

Robert realized that every timeline communicates priorities, whether leaders intend it or not. When dates are missed repeatedly, teams stop believing in leadership. Harvard Business Review notes that organizations often normalize unrealistic timelines because speed is mistaken for competence [2]. Robert had done precisely that.

He reset expectations by grounding timelines. He broke work into phases, implementing planning, preparation, execution, and follow-up for each phase. Each receiving time is based on evidence rather than optimism. This aligned with PMI guidance that schedules should be developed based on validated assumptions, resource availability, and historical performance, not solely on pressure [12].

Making Time Visible

Robert discovered that time was invisible until it failed. Tasks took longer than expected because no one had measured them before. He tracked how long activities took, including meetings, approvals, onboarding, and follow-ups. The data was uncomfortable but clarifying.

Once time became visible, decisions improved. Deadlines became credible. Staff no longer felt like they were constantly behind. PMI emphasizes that realistic duration estimates are essential to sustainable delivery and stakeholder confidence [12].

Sequencing Work Instead of Stacking It

Another mistake Robert corrected was stacking tasks instead of sequencing them. He had assumed parallel work meant faster progress; in reality, it created bottlenecks and mistakes. Research on workflow efficiency confirms that unmanaged task overlap increases delays and reduces quality [7]. Robert redesigned the timeline so critical tasks happened in sequence, not in competition. Dependencies were acknowledged rather than ignored; the result was that different systems flowed as designed rather than collided with each other.

Aligning Timelines to the Target Population

Timeline management also changed once Robert aligned schedules to the target population's reality. He stopped planning based on organizational convenience and started designing around participant availability and behavior. Research on communication and engagement shows that timing significantly affects participation and follow-through [8]. Sessions were scheduled when participants could attend consistently. Follow-ups were timed to when people were most responsive. When this change was implemented, Robert saw a significant decrease in attrition.

Using Incremental Milestones

Instead of setting distant end dates, Robert built short, achievable milestones. Research on incremental improvement shows that progress is more sustainable when change is broken into small, consistent steps rather than significant, disruptive shifts [10]. Each milestone created momentum. Progress was visible.

Building Buffers Without Apology

Robert also learned to protect time. He built buffers into the schedule for delays, decision-making, and recovery. PMI emphasizes that risk-aware scheduling includes contingency planning to absorb disruption without collapsing delivery [12]. At first, this felt uncomfortable because buffers mirrored inefficiency, but they were crucial in reducing crises. Work finished on time more often because the timeline respected reality.

Communicating the Timeline Clearly

Finally, Robert focused on communication. A timeline only works if everyone understands it. Learning & Development Quarterly highlights that multi-channel communication improves adherence to schedules by reducing assumptions and misinterpretations [8]. Robert shared timelines visually, verbally, and in writing. Changes were communicated early. Expectations were explicit. Trust improved because surprises decreased.

Blueprint for the Reader

Robert's approach can be replicated:

1. Treat timelines as commitments [2]
2. Base schedules on actual time data [12]
3. Sequence work to reduce collisions and rework [7]
4. Align timing to participant behavior [8]
5. Use short milestones to sustain momentum [10]
6. Build buffers to absorb disruption without crisis [12]
7. Communicate timelines clearly and consistently [8]

PART II: ESTABLISH

"Establish" is about creating structure, roles, and processes that align with the organization's goals and priorities.

The Goal

Initial goals are not meant to impress stakeholders; they are intended to guide action. According to Locke and Latham's goal-setting theory, specific and moderately challenging goals significantly increase performance [1]. The problem is that many leaders hear 'challenging' and translate it as 'heroic.' Robert made this mistake by confusing goals with wishes. A wish says, 'It would be great if this happened.' A goal says, 'This will happen, and here is exactly what it will take.'

Programs collapse under vague goals. If the goal, for example, is 'improve outreach,' congratulations, you have said absolutely nothing. Improve how? For whom? By when? Using what resources? Robert discovered that unclear goals lead to unclear actions, and unclear actions lead to poor overall performance.

Robert also learned that initial goals must be limited, referring to the adage, "the only way to eat an elephant is one bite at a time." Programs implode when they begin with fifteen goals, mostly because nobody can name all fifteen without reading from a script. Research shows that humans can effectively manage three to five major priorities at once [2]. Anything more becomes noise. Robert limited his initial goals to four: launch the program, recruit participants, establish workflows, and collect baseline data. Simple, straightforward, and solution-focused.'

By grounding his goals in clarity and realism, Robert avoided the trap most leaders fall into. Initial goals do not need to change the world; they need to change the next 30 to 90 days. Programs succeed through momentum. And momentum is the natural outcome of well-chosen goals.

Robert's journey with initial goal setting taught him something fundamental: programs do not need extravagant goals; they need functional ones. Goals that move things forward, guide decisions, and create early wins. Those early wins build confidence, and confidence builds culture. And culture, as every leader eventually learns, is what carries a program farther than any goal ever could.

Application: How Robert Applied Goal Setting in Practice

For Robert, goal setting did not begin as a careful exercise in execution. It started as an ambition. His early goals were bold, inspirational, and wildly unrealistic. One early draft even included the phrase *"dramatically transform the community,"* which sounded impressive until he realized it translated to absolutely nothing actionable.

This is a common trap. New program managers often treat goal setting as a branding exercise rather than a leadership responsibility. Robert assumed that big goals would inspire considerable effort. What he learned instead was that vague ambition creates confusion, not motivation.

According to Locke and Latham's goal-setting theory, performance increases most when goals are specific and moderately challenging, rather than heroic or abstract [3]. Robert initially latched onto the word *'challenging' and ignored the word 'specifically'*. He confused goals with wishes. A wish says, *"It would be great if this happened."* A goal says, *"This will happen, and here is exactly what it requires."*

The consequences of vague goals appeared quickly. Staff interpreted priorities differently. Meetings drifted, and progress was difficult to explain, let alone measure. When the goal was "improve outreach," no one knew what success looked like. Improve how? For whom? By when? With what resources? As Robert later joked, unclear goals led to unclear actions, which in turn led to staff frustration and a decline in trust in his ability to lead.

Harvard Business Review research reinforces this pattern, noting that organizations often fail early not because of poor execution, but because leaders fail to define problems and goals precisely enough to guide action [2]. Robert realized his program was not behind; it was undefined.

Applying for the Three Realities Test

The turning point came when Robert stopped asking what *sounded* right and started asking what was *real*. He created what he called The Three Realities Test, a simple filter every initial goal had to pass:

1. Is this achievable with the resources I have?

2. Can this be measured easily?

3. Will this make a meaningful difference for the target population?

These questions immediately eliminated more than half of Robert's original goals, which turned out to be a relief rather than a loss. What remained were goals that were easily managed, measured, and understood. This aligns with PMI's guidance that early program success depends on aligning objectives with current capabilities and constraints, rather than on future assumptions [1].

Limiting Goals to Create Momentum

Robert also learned that the number of goals mattered as much as their quality. Programs often implode at launch because leaders attempt to pursue too many priorities simultaneously. Organizational development research shows that minor, consistent improvements outperform broad, sweeping reforms, especially in initial stages [10]. Humans can only manage a limited number of major priorities effectively before focus degrades. Robert put this into practice when he had the opportunity to launch a new program that supported people with physical disabilities in the community.

Robert limited his initial goals to five that were achieved in order:

- Collect baseline data.
- Develop resources required based on data.
- Establish workflows.
- Launch program.

These goals were not flashy. They were functional. And that made them powerful. By narrowing the focus, Robert gave the team clarity. Everyone could articulate the goals without referencing notes. Progress could be seen weekly. Momentum replaced anxiety.

Using Goals as Decision Filters

Once goals were defined, Robert used them as filters for decision-making. New ideas were not evaluated solely on enthusiasm. They were evaluated based on alignment. If an initiative did not support one of the five goals, it did not move forward. This prevented early scope creep and preserved limited resources, a practice PMI identifies as essential to program stability [12]. Goals stopped being statements of intent and became tools for leadership.

Measuring Progress Without Paralysis

Measurement was another lesson. Robert initially overcomplicated metrics, creating tracking systems that generated more frustration than insight. He simplified. Each goal had one or two indicators that mattered. Progress was visible without being overwhelming.

This approach reflected Locke and Latham's emphasis on feedback as a critical component of effective goal systems [3]. Feedback was not about punishment; it was about adjustment.

Blueprint for the Reader

Robert's approach to goal setting can be replicated:

1. Replace inspirational language with specific, actionable outcomes [3]
2. Test goals against current resources and constraints [1]
3. Limit initial goals to three to five priorities to preserve focus [10]
4. Use goals as decision filters, not just benchmarks [12]
5. Measure progress consistently to support learning [3]

Robert learned that programs do not need visionary goals at launch. They need functional ones. Goals that move work forward, guide decisions, and create early wins. Those early wins build confidence. Confidence builds culture. And culture, more than any single goal, is what carries a program forward.

Staffing & Volunteer Needs

Adequate staffing requires matching tasks to strengths, not to availability. Research on organizational performance shows that employees who use their strengths daily are significantly more productive and less likely to experience burnout [1]. This forced Robert to evaluate his team honestly: they thrived on details, excelled at relationships, could manage chaos without combusting, and were fully capable of complex decision-making.

Volunteers added another layer of complexity. Volunteers are wonderful, but they are not free labor; they are unpaid partners. They require clarity, training, and meaningful roles. Robert learned the hard way that assigning volunteers to tasks they were not equipped to do created more work, not less. His early strategy of 'Let's plug this volunteer in anywhere' led directly to a spectacularly disorganized event, with misplaced supplies, three duplicate sign-in sheets, and a missing table later found in the parking lot.

The solution came in the form of structured onboarding and role definition. Volunteers were assigned specific roles with clear expectations, training materials, and a point of contact for questions. This improved performance immediately and reduced the number of times Robert had to say, 'That's okay, let's try something different next time,' a phrase he had been repeating far too often.

Another lesson Robert learned was the importance of redundancy in staffing. Programs that rely on one key person for critical tasks are waiting for disaster to strike. Cross-training staff and volunteers ensures that no single absence could derail operations. It also prevented the infamous 'single point of failure,' which, according to Murphy's Law, always occurs at the worst possible moment [2].

Finally, Robert realized that people need support systems, not just assignments. Clear communication channels, regular check-ins, and reasonable workloads prevented burnout and frustration. When staff feel valued, and volunteers feel purposeful, programs thrive. When they do not, programs limp along until someone eventually asks, 'Why does everything feel harder than it should?'

In the end, adequate staffing is not solely about filling slots; it is about building a team that can consistently execute the program's mission. Robert learned that when people are placed where they perform best, the program becomes much stronger.

Staffing Plan Application

Robert's earliest staffing plan was simple and deeply flawed: fill every role as quickly as possible and trust that passion would compensate for inexperience, overload, and ambiguity. On paper, the program looked fully staffed. In practice, it felt fragile. People burned out quickly. Volunteers disappeared without explanation. Staff spent more time covering gaps than delivering outcomes.

What Robert eventually realized was that the staffing problems were not people problems. They were design problems. The Project Management Institute emphasizes that program performance depends on aligning human resources with defined scope, timelines, and objectives—not optimism or goodwill [1]. Robert had done the opposite. He recruited people first and figured out what they would do later. The result was confusion and misalignment.

Defining Work Before Recruiting People

Robert started by mapping tasks instead of roles. Every recurring activity was listed, along with its frequency, skill requirement, and tolerance for error. PMI guidance stresses that role clarity reduces dependency risk and prevents burnout by aligning responsibility with capacity [12]. Robert saw immediately how much work had been informally assigned without ownership.

Some tasks required reliability, others, flexibility. And a few required specialized skills. Treating all staffing needs as interchangeable has created unnecessary stress. Once work was defined, staffing decisions became easier and more effective.

Separating Staff Roles from Volunteer Roles

One of Robert's most important lessons was learning what *not* to give volunteers. Early on, volunteers were placed into roles that required consistency, accountability, and decision-making authority. When volunteers missed shifts or were disengaged, the program suffered.

Research on workflow efficiency shows that systems fail when critical processes depend on inconsistent inputs [7]. Robert stopped assigning volunteers to roles that could not tolerate disruption. Paid staff handled continuity. Volunteers supported expansion. These changes stabilized operations immediately and significantly increased morale and understanding.

Recruiting for Fit, Not Availability

Robert also realized that availability was a poor substitute for qualifications. Volunteers were often eager but misaligned. Staff were capable but overstretched. Organizational research shows that performance improves when individuals are placed in roles aligned with their strengths and expectations [3].

Robert rewrote role descriptions in plain language:

- What are the roles and responsibilities?
- How often is this role needed?
- What support is provided?

People are self-selected more accurately. Fewer recruits dropped out. The people who remained were initially more closely aligned.

Limiting Roles to Preserve Sustainability

At one point, Robert counted over twenty informal roles supporting the program. No one could name them all. Organizational development research confirms that excessive role complexity reduces accountability and increases failure rates [10]. Robert consolidated roles into a smaller, more transparent structure. Fewer roles did not mean less help; they meant clearer ownership and more understanding. Staff stopped duplicating effort, volunteers understood boundaries, and coordination improved.

Building Redundancy Without Burnout

Robert also addressed single-point dependency. Some tasks were performed by only one person, with no contingency. When that person was unavailable, everything stalled. PMI emphasizes that programs must avoid single-resource dependency to reduce operational risk [12].

Robert cross-trained selectively, not everyone on everything, but enough redundancy to prevent collapse. This reduced stress and increased resilience.

Supporting Volunteers Through Structure

Volunteers did not fail because they lacked commitment. They failed because expectations were unclear. Learning & Development Quarterly highlights that multi-channel communication and clear onboarding improve retention in nonprofit programs [8]—Robert standardized onboarding, check-ins, and feedback. Volunteers stayed longer because they knew what was expected and felt supported.

Using Feedback to Adjust Staffing Models

Robert treated staffing as dynamic by regularly soliciting feedback from staff and volunteers. Research on feedback shows that teams perform better when leaders actively adjust systems based on lived experience [5]. Roles were refined, schedules adjusted, and staffing became strategic rather than reactive.

Blueprint for the Reader

Robert's staffing approach can be replicated:

1. Define work before roles [12]

2. Separate staff responsibilities based on reliability needs [7]
3. Limit roles to reduce complexity and confusion [10]
4. Build redundancy to eliminate single-point failure [12]
5. Support volunteers with structure and communication [8]
6. Use feedback to refine staffing models [5] continuously!

Robert did not fix staffing by finding better people. He fixed it by building a better structure for the people he had. Once staffing aligned with organizational needs, the program stopped feeling fragile and started feeling dependable.

Communication Plan

If program management had a list of unavoidable truths, the first one would be this: Poor communication will break your program faster than anything else. Robert discovered this when he walked into a meeting where half the team thought a deadline was next week, the other half thought it was last week, and one person did not know a deadline existed at all. Chaos, it turns out, does not come from incompetence. It comes from people operating with different information.

A communication plan is not optional. It is the operating manual for how information moves through a program. Without one, teams fall into the well-documented trap of assumption-based communication: the dangerous belief that people know what you meant, even if you never actually said it. Studies show that nearly 70% of organizational mistakes can be traced back to poor communication flow [1]. Unfortunately, Robert learned this statistic, as most do, the hard way.

The first step in creating a communication plan is to identify your program's communication needs. Robert started by listing every recurring piece of information the team needed: schedule updates, policy changes, task assignments, progress reports, partner updates, and the occasional motivational memo to prevent existential despair during busy seasons.

Next came the method. Robert realized that not all communication should use the same channel. Critical updates needed an email; quick clarifications were better suited for chat platforms; and weekly overviews belonged in team meetings—anything longer than three paragraphs should always be put in a document. Anything emotional requires face-to-face discussion. And absolutely nothing ever should be communicated solely through sticky notes left on the breakroom fridge, a mistake the team was unfortunately familiar with.

Robert also implemented a simple rule: every communication needed an owner. When 'Everyone' is responsible for sharing information, no one does. Assigning point people for task updates, data tracking, and partner communication transformed confusion into clarity. Accountability made information flow predictable.

One of Robert's most significant breakthroughs was learning the value of communication cadence, the scheduled rhythm for how often information is shared. Weekly briefings, daily check-ins, monthly progress reviews, and quarterly planning sessions created a predictable pattern that staff could rely on. Research supports this approach, showing that organizations with consistent communication rhythms experience higher levels of trust and stronger team cohesion [2].

Finally, Robert recognized the importance of upward communication. Leaders often assume that if no one is complaining, everything is fine. This is false. Silence is not the absence of problems; it is the absence of safe communication. Encouraging staff and volunteers to voice concerns early allowed the team to address issues before they evolved into crises.

A communication plan is not about sending more messages. It is about sending the right messages to the right people at the right time. When this happens, teams work together much better. When it does not, you get misalignment, resentment, confusion, and at least one person who insists they were never told about the thing everyone else remembers discussing.

By establishing a consistent, intentional communication structure, Robert turned information from a liability into one of the program's biggest strengths. In program management, communication is not just a tool; it is the infrastructure on which everything else rests.

Applying the Communication Plan

Robert learned the hard way that communication does not fail because people are inattentive. It fails because leaders assume clarity exists when it does not. Early in the program, Robert believed that information shared was information understood. Emails were sent, updates were put out in meetings, and silence was always interpreted as agreement. What he did not realize was whether that silence was often meant to confusion, not consent.

The Project Management Institute identifies ineffective communication as one of the most persistent causes of program inefficiency, especially in environments with mixed staff, volunteers, and partners [1]. Robert saw this play out repeatedly. Tasks were completed incorrectly, deadlines were missed, and people were frustrated or burnt out.

So, Robert changed the framing.

Instead of asking, *"Did we communicate this?"*
He asked, *"How would someone experience this information if this were their first day?"*

That shift placed a heavy focus on clarity, simplicity, and effectiveness in program communication.

Designing Communication Around Roles, Not Hierarchy

One of Robert's earliest mistakes was assuming that organizational charts dictated the flow of communication. Vital information traveled upward efficiently but drifted downward unevenly. Volunteers often learned about changes late, if at all, and partners received updates without context.

Research on multi-channel communication shows that it is most effective when designed around role-specific needs rather than hierarchical structure [8]. Robert mapped communication by function:

- Who needs to act?
- Who needs awareness?
- Who needs confirmation?

Once messages were designed around action, confusion dropped, and productivity increased dramatically.

Reducing Information to What Actually Matters

Robert also learned that too much communication was just as harmful as too little. Long emails went unread. Meetings ran long without producing clarity. Harvard Business Review notes that organizations often bury critical information under excess detail, causing people to miss what matters [2].

Robert adopted a rule: if a message could not be summarized in three sentences, it was not ready to be sent. Supporting details were optional, never required. This disciplined restraint improved comprehension and response rates overnight.

Matching Channels to Message Type

Not every message belonged in the same place. Robert separated communication by purpose:

- Direction went in writing.
- Coordination lived in shared tools
- Changes were communicated clearly in memos or policy updates.
- Feedback was organized through structured check-ins.

Learning & Development Quarterly emphasizes that multi-channel reinforcement improves retention and reduces misinterpretation, especially in nonprofit and volunteer-driven programs [8]. Robert stopped relying on memory and started relying on systems.

Timing Communication to Reduce Risk

Many of the program's earlier problems were not caused by bad decisions, but by bad communication. PMI highlights that proactive communication reduces operational risk by preventing misalignment before it impacts outcomes [12]. Robert began communicating earlier than he felt comfortable, sending draft timelines and flagging potential changes before final decisions were made. This transparency reduced anxiety rather than increasing it. People adjusted their expectations early rather than waiting to react.

Building Confirmation into the Plan

Robert stopped assuming understanding; instead, he built confirmation into communication. Staff summarized the following steps, volunteers acknowledged receipt, and partners confirmed expectations. Organizational Behavior Institute research shows that feedback loops improve execution by closing the gap between intent and understanding [5]. This was not micromanagement; it was ensuring proper communication that highlighted complete comprehension.

Protecting Attention by Creating Predictability

One of the most powerful changes Robert made was predictability. Communication arrived when expected, in consistent formats, through known channels. PMI's global research highlights that predictability strengthens trust and engagement in complex programs [1]. People stopped scanning every message for urgency. When something mattered, they knew.

Adjusting Communication Through Feedback

Robert treated communication as a living system. He asked what was unclear, what felt excessive, and what was missing. Feedback revealed blind spots that leadership often overlooked [5]. Adjustments were made incrementally rather than reactively and communication improved without becoming louder.

Blueprint for the Reader

Robert's communication plan can be replicated:

1. Design communication around roles and actions, not hierarchy [8]
2. Reduce messages to essential information only [2]
3. Communicate early to reduce risk and confusion [12]
4. Build confirmation loops to ensure understanding [5]
5. Create predictable communication rhythms to protect attention [1]
6. Refine communication continuously through feedback [5]

Once communication became intentional rather than habitual, the program stopped guessing and started moving together.

Physical Space Needs

Physical space is an essential part of every program, rarely acknowledged, frequently blamed, and always underestimated. This became apparent when Robert attempted to conduct a workshop for twenty people in a room that comfortably seated eight. The result was an uncomfortable, cluttered, and underwhelming execution of a fantastic concept. Physical space matters because humans require it to function, and programs require it to operate without violating fire codes.

Many leaders assume space planning is a logistical afterthought. It is a structural priority. The design, size, layout, and accessibility of a program's physical environment directly influence participation, flow, safety, and satisfaction. Studies in environmental psychology show that physical space impacts behavior, stress levels, and engagement far more than most managers realize [1].

Robert's experience taught him that properly planning physical space needs is often the simplest way to enhance a program without spending a fortune.

Physical Space Needs (Application)

Robert used to think physical space was a logistical detail, something you secured after the real planning was done. If there were chairs, a table, and enough room for people to gather, the space felt "good enough." What he eventually learned was that space is never neutral. It either supports the work mission or it works against it.

The Environmental Psychology Review makes clear that physical environments directly influence behavior, attention, stress, and productivity [6]. Robert did not encounter this insight in a journal; he experienced it through distracted participants, strained conversations, and sessions that felt harder than they needed to be. The work had not changed. The space had.

Recognizing Space as Part of the Program System

Robert's first realization was that physical space is an active part of the system that cannot be overlooked. PMI's global research emphasizes that operational conditions, including facilities and infrastructure, must align with program objectives for outcomes to be sustainable [1]. Robert saw that his program goals demanded focus, safety, and interaction, while his spaces communicated transience and compromise.

Designing Space Around the Target Population

Once the target population was clearly defined, space decisions became easier. Robert stopped choosing spaces solely based on availability and began selecting them based on participant needs. Environmental psychology research shows that comfort, accessibility, and layout significantly affect engagement and willingness to participate [6].

For some participants, privacy mattered. For others, accessibility and visibility mattered more. Robert adjusted room selection, layout, and flow accordingly. These were not expensive changes, but they were intentional. The results showed that participants stayed longer, conversations deepened, and, surprisingly, attendance became more consistent.

Reducing Environmental Barriers

Robert also learned to look for barriers hidden in plain sight: long walking distances, poor signage, and other access obstacles. Workplace efficiency research confirms that physical barriers increase cognitive load and reduce performance, even when people are motivated [7].

Once the proper space was established, Robert focused on removing clutter and standardizing layouts. These simple adjustments reduced frustration and freed energy for actual engagement.

Aligning Space with Program Activities

Another mistake Robert made was using one space for every purpose. Reflection, instruction, collaboration, and de-escalation all require different spatial conditions. PMI emphasizes that aligning resources, including physical environments, to task requirements improves execution quality [12].

Robert designated spaces by function whenever possible. Quiet spaces for sensitive conversations. Open spaces for collaboration. Clear exists for safety and comfort. The program stopped fighting its environment and started working with it.

Supporting Safety and Psychological Comfort

Physical space also affected safety, both physical and psychological. Poor lighting, crowded layouts, and unclear exits increased anxiety. Organizational research shows that perceived unsafe environments reduce participation and trust [5].

Robert improved lighting, clarified exits, and ensured staff visibility. He also paid attention to how spaces felt emotionally. Calm replaced tension once the space design matched the intent.

Making Space Predictable

Consistency mattered; participants felt more comfortable when layouts were familiar. Research in Environmental Psychology Review highlights that predictable environments reduce stress and improve focus [6]. Robert standardized room setups, so participants did not have to reorient themselves each visit. Predictability, he learned, is a form of respect.

Evaluating Space Through Feedback

Robert did not assume space changes worked. He asked. Feedback revealed distractions he had overlooked and comforts he underestimated. Organizational Behavior Institute research confirms that feedback systems surface environmental issues that leadership often misses [5].

Blueprint for the Reader

Robert's approach to physical space needs can be replicated:

1. Treat physical space as an active part of the program system [1]
2. Design space around target population needs, not availability [6]
3. Remove environmental barriers that drain attention and energy [7]
4. Align spaces to specific activities and outcomes [12]
5. Support safety and psychological comfort through design [5]
6. Create consistency to reduce stress and cognitive load [6]
7. Use feedback to refine space decisions continuously [5]

Safety Planning

Safety planning is the part of program management that everyone agrees is essential, yet most will avoid until something goes wrong. Robert learned this lesson when a routine program was abruptly interrupted by what he later described as 'an incident involving a spilled drink, a slippery floor, one overly energetic volunteer, and a series of events that unfolded like a slow-motion documentary about poor decisions.' No one was seriously hurt, but the moment was clarifying. Safety is not optional; it is operational.

Most leaders imagine safety in extreme medical emergencies, violent incidents, and severe weather. While those events do matter, research shows that over 80% of program safety failures stem from everyday hazards: trip risks, miscommunication, unsupervised activities, overworked staff, and unclear procedures [1]. During his first safety audit, Robert quickly realized that most of the risks identified could have been prevented with a simple checklist and 10 minutes of forethought.

Safety planning begins with one question: 'What could go wrong here?' It is not a pessimistic exercise; it is a professional one. Robert walked through each program space with a clipboard, documenting hazards such as unstable furniture, blocked exits, unsecured supplies, inconsistent sign-in processes, and a chair that made a mysterious clicking sound whenever someone sat in it. Identifying hazards is only step one; addressing them is step two. He learned that even minor corrections, such as reorganizing storage, marking wet floors, or clarifying emergency exits, significantly reduced risk.

Next came staff readiness. A safety plan is only helpful if people follow it. Robert created simple, scenario-based guides rather than long, procedural documents no one would read. Staff were trained in basic emergency responses, conflict de-escalation, facility lockdown procedures, and incident reporting. Volunteers were given a shorter version tailored to their roles. This kept the program compliant while avoiding information overload.

Communication during emergencies was another critical element. Robert established safety roles so that decisions did not devolve into a debate committee during high-pressure moments. He also implemented a multi-channel notification system, text alerts, email notices, and posted signage to ensure critical messages reached everyone quickly.

Robert also prioritized participant safety. This included privacy protection, safe participant check-in systems, and appropriate supervision ratios. He worked closely with staff to ensure boundaries and expectations were clear. He learned quickly that assumptions create risk, especially when working with vulnerable populations. Clear rules keep everyone safe.

Finally, Robert realized that safety is cultural. Programs thrive when safety becomes a shared responsibility rather than a manager's chore. Staff began proactively reporting hazards, volunteers reminded each other of protocols, and participants engaged more responsibly because the environment felt orderly and predictable.

Safety planning does not eliminate risk, but it dramatically reduces unnecessary workplace injuries. Robert discovered that the most effective safety plans are simple, proactive, consistently reinforced, and easy to execute. Programs that treat safety as a living system, not a binder collecting dust, are programs built to last.

Safety Planning (Application)

Robert did not initially think of safety planning as leadership work. He thought of it as paperwork, necessary, dull, and theoretical. Safety lived in binders, policies, and briefings that everyone acknowledged but few truly absorbed. The program "had a plan," which Robert believed was the same thing as being prepared; It was not.

The wake-up call came not from a significant incident, but from a near miss. A situation that should have been routine unfolded into a tense scramble due to confusion about roles, escalation steps, and communication channels. No one was hurt, but everyone was shaken. Robert realized something unsettling: the program had safety documents but lacked *safety readiness*.

PMI research shows that programs are most vulnerable when risks are known in theory but not in practice, especially in environments involving people, volunteers, and external partners [1]. Robert saw himself squarely in that description. So, he changed the way he approached safety.

Instead of asking, *"Do we have a safety plan?"*
Robert asked, *"Would people know exactly what to do if something went wrong today?"*

Treating Safety as an Operational System

Robert's first adjustment was conceptual. Safety was not a policy; it was a system that had to function under stress. Harvard Business Review notes that organizations often fail to identify problems early because warning signs are normalized and contingency plans are not operationalized [2]. Robert recognized that his team had normalized uncertainty.

He reframed safety planning around real scenarios rather than compliance checklists. What happens if a participant becomes distressed? If a conflict escalates? If a Volunteer has a medical emergency? These were not hypothetical; they were patterns. Once safety was framed as part of daily operations, people stopped seeing it as extra work and began to see it as a shared responsibility.

Clarifying Roles Before Emergencies

One of the most significant risks Robert identified was role ambiguity. In stressful situations, people hesitate when unsure who should act. PMI emphasizes that unclear responsibility increases response time and amplifies risk during incidents [12]. Robert addressed this by clearly and visibly defining safety roles.

Who makes the call?
Who contacts external support?
Who documents the incident?
Who communicates with participants?

This reduced hesitation and eliminated the dangerous pause that occurs when everyone waits for someone else to move.

Designing Safety Around the Target Population

Safety planning became more effective once Robert aligned it with the target population. Different populations carry different risks, triggers, and needs. PMI's global research emphasizes that risk mitigation must be contextual rather than generic [1]. Robert adapted safety responses to reflect the realities of the program's population.

That meant adjusting environments, supervision levels, communication tone, and escalation thresholds. Safety stopped being theoretical and became relevant.

Training for Recognition, Not Reaction

Robert also learned that most safety failures occur before a formal incident begins. Subtle cues, behavior changes, rising tension, and withdrawal often go unnoticed. Organizational research shows that feedback-rich environments identify risks earlier and respond more effectively [5].

Robert trained staff and volunteers to recognize early warning signs rather than wait for crises. This did not require advanced training. It required attention, permission to speak up, and a straightforward escalation process without fear of overreacting.

Building Redundancy into Safety Systems

One of Robert's earlier mistakes was relying on a single "safety person." If that person was absent, uncertainty returned. PMI emphasizes that single-point dependency increases operational risk across programs [12]. Robert built redundancy deliberately.

Multiple people knew the plan. Backups were identified. Safety responsibilities were shared rather than siloed, reducing stress and improving confidence across the team.

Communicating Safety Expectations Clearly

Safety planning also requires communication discipline. Learning & Development Quarterly highlights that multi-channel communication improves understanding in high-stress contexts [8]. Robert ensured safety expectations were communicated verbally, reinforced in writing, and practiced periodically. People did not need to memorize policies. They needed to know where to find guidance and who to contact.

Reviewing and Refining Through Incidents and Feedback

After any incident, no matter how small, Robert reviewed what happened. Not to assign blame, but to improve systems. Organizational research shows that incremental improvements following real events lead to more resilient organizations than infrequent, large-scale reforms [10]. Each review refined the safety plan, confidence grew, and fear decreased.

Blueprint for the Reader

Robert's approach to safety planning can be replicated:

1. Treat safety as an operational system, not a document [1]
2. Clarify roles and escalation paths before stress occurs [12]
3. Design safety responses around the target population [1]
4. Train people to recognize early warning signs, not just emergencies [5]
5. Build redundancy to eliminate single-point dependency [12]
6. Communicate safety expectations clearly and repeatedly [8]
7. Refine safety plans through real-world feedback, not assumptions [10]

Robert did not make the program safer by adding rules. He made it safer by making safety actionable.

PART III ELEVATE

"Elevate" focuses on improvement, feedback, and all the adjustments that turn your business or program into something you are proud of

What's Working

One of the most overlooked skills in program management is the ability to recognize what is working. Not what is loud, not what is urgent, and certainly not what is shiny, just what's functioning well. Robert learned this when he realized that his team spent so much time fixing problems that they forgot to notice the systems that were holding the entire operation together with remarkable consistency.

In many programs, success hides in plain sight. Smooth check-ins, returning participants, and volunteers who show up early and often create a process that operates so predictably that nobody even thinks about it. These are signs that something is working. And according to organizational research, teams that regularly identify successful processes experience higher performance and stronger morale [1].

Robert discovered that identifying what's working is not about celebrating wins; it is about understanding why they are working and how those elements can be replicated. During his first review cycle, he created a list titled 'Unexpected Successes,' which included everything from improved attendance to the functioning of a previously unreliable scheduling system. The exercise revealed patterns he had never noticed.

For example, one of the program's most successful workshops achieved high satisfaction scores despite being planned at the last minute. Robert initially chalked this up to luck, but further analysis showed that the facilitator was naturally engaging, the format was interactive, and the content directly matched participant needs. None of these elements required luck; they required understanding.

Another win came from a simple communication habit: weekly recap emails. Robert discovered that these emails were a stabilizing force, keeping the team aligned even when the week was chaotic. The recap emails were not glamorous, but they were effective. And effectiveness, not glamour, is the backbone of successful programs.

Identifying what is working also highlights where effort was being wasted. Robert noticed that some initiatives produced minimal results despite consuming considerable time and energy, while smaller, simpler efforts produced outsized impact. This insight allowed him to shift resources strategically instead of emotionally.

The process of finding what works taught Robert that programs do not just succeed through problem-solving; they grow through pattern recognition. When leaders understand the conditions that create success, they can make those conditions repeatable. And when success becomes repeatable, programs become sustainable.

Recognizing what's working is not complacency. It is an act of intelligence. Programs that only focus on what is broken eventually burn out their teams. Programs that study what's effective build momentum. And momentum is the currency of long-term progress.

What's Working (Application)

For Robert, identifying what was working felt almost irresponsible at first. The culture he had inherited was wired to focus on problems. Meetings revolved around gaps, failures, and what still needed to be done. Success was treated as temporary, accidental, or not worth naming because "there's still so much to fix." Robert realized that the mindset was not humble; it was inefficient.

Programs do not improve by ignoring success. They improve by understanding it.

PMI research highlights that high-performing programs intentionally analyze successful practices to reinforce and scale them, rather than constantly reinventing solutions [1]. Robert saw the opposite happening. Wins were happening quietly while problems received all the attention.

So, he changed the question.

Instead of asking, *"What's broken?"*
Robert asked, *"What is already working, and why?"*

That shift changed morale, clarity, and momentum almost immediately.

Separating Real Wins from Lucky Outcomes

Robert's first task was to distinguish between success driven by sound systems and success driven by luck. A full session did not automatically mean the program was effective. It might suggest a good day, a strong referral, or favorable timing.

Harvard Business Review notes that organizations often misinterpret isolated positive outcomes as proof of effectiveness without understanding the underlying drivers [2]. Robert did not want false confidence. He wanted repeatable success.

When evaluating luck vs. system quality, Robert examined attendance patterns, completion rates, feedback, and staff workload related to successful activities. What he found surprised him: the most successful components shared common traits. They had clear ownership. Expectations were explicit. Communication was simple. Timing matched participant availability. Success was not random. It was designed.

Using Feedback to Identify Strengths

Robert then turned to feedback, not just complaints, but patterns of satisfaction. Organizational Behavior Institute research shows that feedback systems are equally valuable for identifying strengths as they are for identifying problems [5]. Robert asked staff, volunteers, and participants a simple question:
"What feels easiest or most effective right now?"

The answers were consistent. Certain workflows flowed naturally. Some communication methods worked better than others. A few staff roles felt sustainable rather than draining. Robert documented these strengths instead of assuming they would persist on their own.

Protecting What Works from Overload

One mistake Robert corrected quickly was overloading successful systems. When something worked well, the instinct was to pile on more responsibility. That usually broke it.

Research on incremental improvement shows that small, consistent successes outperform aggressive scaling efforts, especially in program development [10]. Robert resisted the urge to expand immediately. He stabilized first.

He asked:
- What conditions allow this to work?
- What resources are required?
- What would break it?

Only after those questions were answered did he consider expansion.

Standardizing Without Killing Flexibility

Robert also learned that documenting what works does not mean freezing it. PMI emphasizes that standardization should support consistency while allowing adaptation [12]. Robert documented best practices as guidelines, not rigid rules.

This allowed new staff and volunteers to replicate success without having to strive for experienced team members' autonomy. What worked became teachable instead of tribal knowledge.

Using What's Working to Build Confidence

Momentum matters. PMI's global research shows that early and visible successes build confidence and stakeholder trust, thereby improving long-term program performance [1]. Robert made a point of officially naming what was working. This was not cheerleading. It was clarity.

Staff felt seen. Volunteers felt valued. Participants felt reassured that the program was stable. Confidence increased without ignoring reality.

Aligning Resources Toward Proven Success

Once strengths were identified, Robert intentionally aligned resources. Time, attention, and support flowed toward activities that produced consistent outcomes. Underperforming areas were not ignored, but they were not allowed to drain successful systems either. This prevented burnout and protected morale.

Blueprint for the Reader

Robert's approach to identifying what's working can be replicated:

1. Actively analyze successful outcomes, not just failures [1]
2. Separate repeatable systems from lucky moments [2]
3. Use feedback to identify strengths and efficiencies [5]
4. Protect successful practices from overextension [10]
5. Document what works without over-restricting it [12]
6. Reinforce success publicly to build confidence and trust [1]
7. Align resources toward **proven effectiveness**, not assumptions.

Robert did not lower standards by naming success. He raised them by making success repeatable.

What's Not Working

Most programs accumulate dysfunctional elements the same way basements accumulate items: slowly, quietly, and without anyone remembering how those items got there in the first place. Robert found outdated procedures from 2013, unused forms, and a process requiring three signatures, despite no one knowing why. Identifying these issues requires necessary curiosity and courage, two traits that often vanish when leaders fear uncovering more problems than solutions.

Research shows that organizations frequently avoid acknowledging internal failures because doing so challenges comfort, familiarity, and routine [1]. But ignoring dysfunction does not preserve stability; it erodes it. Robert learned that programs do not collapse overnight. They weaken gradually through repeated friction: inefficient workflows, unclear roles, conflicting priorities, and processes that take twice as long as they need to.

Robert began his analysis by walking through each program activity as if he were a new participant. The results were enlightening. He found that many processes were too long and had unclear instructions. Some responsibilities overlapped so awkwardly that staff unintentionally duplicated work. The participant's experience revealed what internal familiarity had previously hidden.

Next, Robert conducted staff interviews. This was where the absolute truth surfaced. Staff openly described areas of confusion, productivity barriers, and policies that seemed to exist solely out of habit. He learned that one internal report took over two hours to compile each week because the data was stored in three separate locations. Another task required multiple phone calls because communication channels were inconsistent. These were not dramatic failures, but they were daily ones.

The most crucial lesson Robert learned was that inefficiencies rarely happen in isolation. They cluster; a poor process in one area creates stress in another, which in turn creates delays, until the entire system feels heavier than it needs to. Mapping these connections was essential for understanding where to intervene.

He also discovered that some issues were not only about systems; they were about behavior. Inconsistent follow-through, unclear expectations, and a habit of 'fixing things on the fly' created avoidable chaos. Addressing boundaries, clarifying responsibilities, and occasionally reminding staff that improvisation is not a sustainable long-term strategy.

Finally, Robert learned that acknowledging what is not working is not about blame; it is about opportunity. Problems reveal precisely where improvement will have the most significant impact. Every inefficiency uncovered became an invitation to strengthen the program. By the time Robert finished his review, he did not feel discouraged; he felt empowered. He finally understood that identifying weaknesses was not a sign of failure. It was the first step in the transformation.

What's Not Working (Application)

For Robert, naming what was not working felt riskier than naming success. Success builds morale. Failure threatens it. Early in the program, he avoided this section altogether, as focusing on problems would discourage staff and volunteers who were already stretched thin. What he learned instead was that silence created far more damage than honesty ever could.

Unaddressed dysfunction does not disappear. It compounds.

PMI's research on program performance makes this clear: programs stall or fail when leaders delay confronting misalignment, inefficiencies, or ineffective processes, especially when those issues are already visible to frontline staff [1]. Robert eventually realized that everyone knew what was not working; they just did not know whether they were allowed to say it.

So, he changed the question.

Instead of asking, *"Why are you not producing results?"*
Robert asked, *"Why isn't this working?"*

That question opened the door to truth.

Identifying Friction Without Assigning Blame

Robert's first rule was simple: identifying what is not working and why. Harvard Business Review notes that organizations often fail to identify problems early because leaders conflate problem acknowledgment with personal failure [2]. Robert had done this himself. He had avoided hard conversations out of fear that they would feel accusatory.

He reframed the discussion around systems rather than people. When attendance dropped, he did not ask who failed to follow up. He wondered whether follow-up was realistic given workloads. When volunteers were disengaged, he did not question commitment. He examined onboarding and role clarity. Once blame was removed, open dialogue increased, morale improved, and productivity improved drastically.

Using Data to Validate What People Felt

Robert learned quickly that frustration alone was not enough. Feelings pointed toward problems, but data confirmed them. PMI emphasizes that effective evaluation requires both qualitative insight and performance data to prevent bias and defensiveness [12].

Robert reviewed timelines, participation trends, missed handoffs, and task completion, and certain processes consistently broke down. Some roles were overloaded, while others were underutilized. Another concern was communication channels, either too redundant or ignored altogether.

The data did not contradict staff concerns; it validated them.

Recognizing Hidden Work and Invisible Failure

One of the most damaging discoveries was invisible work. Staff were compensating for broken systems, staying late, skipping breaks, and solving problems informally. This made the program appear functional while exhausting the people holding it together.

Research on workplace efficiency shows that unmanaged barriers force individuals to absorb system failures personally, leading to burnout and reduced performance over time [7]. Robert realized that what "wasn't working" had been hidden by effort. Once he faced that reality, he stopped praising heroics and started fixing systems.

Limiting the List to What Actually Matters

At one point, Robert had an extensive list of things that were not working. It was overwhelming. Organizational development research warns that attempting to address too many issues at once often results in no meaningful improvement [10]. Robert learned to prioritize.

He asked three questions:

- Does this issue affect outcomes?
- Does it create risk?
- Does it drain people disproportionately?

Only issues that met at least one of those criteria stayed on the list. Everything else was monitored, not attacked.

Creating Psychological Safety for Honest Feedback

People will not name what is not working unless it is safe to do so. Organizational Behavior Institute research emphasizes that teams perform better when feedback is welcomed and acted upon rather than punished or ignored [5]. Robert had to prove that honesty would not backfire.

He listened without defending. He summarized what he heard. He closed the loop by explaining what would and would not change. Trust grew because feedback led to action rather than consequences.

Turning Problems into Improvement Targets

Once issues were identified and prioritized, Robert reframed them as improvement targets rather than failures. Each problem became a design question: *What would this need to look like to work consistently?*

Incremental improvement research shows that small, focused adjustments outperform sweeping reforms, particularly in complex programs [10]. Robert resisted overhauls. He made one change at a time and measured impact.

Some fixes worked immediately. Others did not. But progress was visible, and that mattered.

Blueprint for the Reader

Robert's approach to identifying what is not working can be replicated:

1. Treat problem identification as system analysis, not criticism [2]
2. Validate concerns with data and observation, not assumptions [12]
3. Prioritize issues that affect outcomes, risk, or sustainability [10]
4. Reframe problems as design challenges, not failures [10]
5. Make small, measurable changes and evaluate impact [12]

Feedback

Most leaders assume they know how things are going. They base conclusions on instincts, assumptions, and the occasional overheard hallway conversation. Unfortunately, research shows that leaders are wrong about internal program performance far more often than they believe, sometimes by as much as 60% [1]. Robert was no exception. He felt everything was fine until he heard a conversation between two staff members about a process that he thought everyone loved. Spoiler: they did not.

Effective programs treat feedback as data, not drama. Whether it comes from staff, participants, volunteers, or partners, feedback reveals gaps between what you think is happening and what is happening. Robert knew at this point that negative feedback can sometimes be the most beneficial. It pinpointed friction points before they failed. Positive feedback was equally important; it showed which systems deserved reinforcement.

One of Robert's most successful strategies was establishing multiple pathways for feedback: anonymous surveys, quick verbal check-ins, suggestion boxes, and structured debriefs. This multi-channel approach ensured that even quiet voices contributed. He found that when feedback collection became routine, people felt safer sharing honest information, which improved program transparency and trust.

Feedback also played a significant role in decision-making. Instead of guessing what participants needed or preferred, Robert allowed their responses to guide program adjustments. This prevented unnecessary work, reduced frustration, and increased engagement. Transparency around feedback was equally important. When people saw their input creating fundamental changes, participation increased dramatically.

Finally, Robert learned that feedback strengthens culture. Programs where staff and participants feel heard foster higher morale, greater ownership, and stronger teamwork. Feedback gave his program a shared language, allowing everyone to participate in its evolution rather than passively experience it.

In the end, Robert did not view feedback as criticism. Instead, he used it as his program's navigational tool. Programs that embrace feedback grow; programs that fear it grow stagnant. Feedback is not just important; it is indispensable.

Importance of Feedback (Application)

Robert used to believe feedback was something you asked for when things went wrong. If attendance dropped or a task failed, he would solicit opinions, adjust, and make improvements. When things were working, feedback felt unnecessary, almost intrusive. What he eventually learned was that this mindset delayed learning and amplified blind spots. Feedback is not inherently correct; it is informational.

The Project Management Institute emphasizes that high-performing programs rely on continuous feedback to align execution with objectives, rather than waiting for performance reviews or end-of-cycle evaluations [1]. Robert realized that by treating feedback as episodic, he was depriving the program of one of its most valuable resources: real-time insight. Increasing the number of feedback points changed how people spoke, how decisions were made, and how quickly the program adapted.

Moving Feedback from Event to System

Robert's first adjustment was structural. Implementing multiple feedback opportunities for employees, then tasking that information seriously. Harvard Business Review notes that organizations fail to identify issues early when feedback is informal, inconsistent, or filtered through hierarchy [2]. Robert had been relying on hallway conversations and after-the-fact debriefs.

He embedded feedback into existing rhythms:

- Brief check-ins after activities
- Regular staff reflections tied to goals.
- Volunteer touchpoints focused on clarity and support.
- Participant follow-ups aligned with program milestones

Feedback stopped being optional. It became expected—and safer.

Differentiating Feedback Types

Not all feedback served the same purpose, and Robert learned to intentionally separate them. Organizational research indicates that teams perform better when leaders distinguish between performance, process, and relational feedback rather than blending them [5].

Robert made those distinctions explicit:

- **Performance feedback:** measured outcomes against goals.
- **Process feedback:** identified friction and inefficiencies.
- **Relational feedback:** built trust, clarity, and morale.

This prevented defensiveness. People knew what kind of input was being *requested and why.*

Creating Psychological Safety Around Feedback

Feedback only works when people believe honesty will not cost them. Early on, staff hesitated. Volunteers softened their comments. Participants avoided specifics. Organizational Behavior Institute research confirms that feedback systems fail when psychological safety is absent, regardless of how frequently feedback is requested [5].

Robert addressed this by changing his responses, not his questions. He listened without correcting, summarized before responding, and acknowledged patterns without singling out individuals. Over time, candor increased because consequences decreased.

Using Feedback to Prevent Problems, Not Just Fix Them

One of Robert's most important lessons was that feedback is a risk-management tool. PMI highlights that continuous feedback reduces program risk by identifying misalignment early when adjustments are still inexpensive [12]. Robert began reviewing feedback not just for what happened, but for what *might* happen next.

Small comments revealed emerging issues: confusion about roles, fatigue in specific workflows, and uncertainty about priorities. Addressing this early prevented escalation. Feedback shifted the program from reactive to anticipatory.

Closing the Loop

Nothing kills feedback faster than silence. Robert learned that asking for input without responding to it eroded trust. Learning & Development Quarterly emphasizes that feedback systems are only effective when contributors see evidence that their input influences decisions [8].

Robert closed the loop intentionally. He shared what he heard. He explained what would change, what would not, and why. Even when feedback could not be acted on immediately, people felt respected because it was acknowledged.

Avoiding Feedback Overload

More feedback was not always better. Robert noticed fatigue when too many questions were asked too often. Organizational development research shows that focused, well-timed feedback produces better results than constant data collection [10]. Robert adjusted the frequency and narrowed the questions. Feedback became more precise and actionable.

Using Feedback to Benchmark Progress

Over time, feedback also became a benchmarking tool. Patterns over weeks and months revealed trends. People Analytics research highlights that benchmarking improves performance evaluation when feedback is consistently compared over time, rather than reviewed in isolation [11]. Robert tracked recurring themes and used them to measure improvement beyond simple metrics. Progress became visible and created quantifiable momentum.

Blueprint for the Reader

Robert's approach to feedback can be replicated:

1. Treat feedback as a continuous system, not a corrective event [1]
2. Embed feedback into existing rhythms to normalize honesty [2]
3. Separate performance, process, and relational feedback [5]
4. Build psychological safety through consistent leadership responses [5]
5. Use feedback to prevent risk, not just fix failure [12]
6. Close the loop so contributors see impact [8]

7. Focus questions to avoid fatigue and improve insight [10]
8. Track patterns over time to benchmark progress [11]

Robert did not strengthen the program by demanding more feedback. He strengthened it by making feedback safe, purposeful, and actionable.

Barriers

Barriers are not the dramatic, cinematic obstacles leaders imagine when they first step into a role. Most barriers are small, persistent, and irritating, more like digital pop-up ads than brick walls. Robert discovered this the day he realized his team was not struggling because of a lack of passion or skill. They were struggling because friction points were draining time, energy, and morale before work even began.

Barriers fall into three common categories: structural, behavioral, and environmental. Structural barriers are built into systems, poor workflows, outdated policies, redundant approval steps, or inconsistent tools. Behavioral barriers stem from habits, communication gaps, or unspoken expectations. Environmental barriers are those delightful conditions outside your control, funding shifts, community trends, partner inconsistencies, or the occasional technological failures that occur precisely when you need to print something important.

Research shows that unaddressed barriers reduce program efficiency by up to 40% [1]. Robert did not need to study to prove he saw it firsthand. A simple task, like onboarding a new participant, required four forms, three separate conversations, and the ceremonial retrieval of a binder no one had opened since 2019. Barriers turn simple actions into adventures nobody asked for.

Robert began identifying barriers by asking his team one question: "What slows you down?" The answers poured out. Confusing processes. Missing information. Delayed decisions. Limited resources. Tools that worked only on alternate Tuesdays. These were not catastrophic problems; they were cumulative ones. Together, they created an environment where everything took longer than necessary.

Participant feedback added another layer of insight. Barriers from the user's perspective included unclear instructions, limited accessibility, long wait times, and inconsistent follow-through. These issues did not reflect a lack of effort; they reflected systemic obstacles that had not yet been acknowledged. Robert learned that when participants struggle to engage, it is rarely their fault.

One of Robert's most impactful discoveries was that removing barriers often required surprisingly minor fixes. Eliminating redundant steps, consolidating information in one location, clarifying who owned which task, or simply redesigning a form transformed workflow efficiency almost immediately. These changes did not require more funding; they required awareness.

Robert also learned that some barriers were cultural. Staff hesitated to raise concerns because they did not want to appear negative. Volunteers avoided asking questions because they did not want to seem unprepared. Participants gave vague responses instead of honest input. Creating a culture where people felt safe naming obstacles enabled the team to solve problems early rather than react late.

The goal of barrier identification is not perfection; it is to establish a sustainable state of efficiency. Programs operate best when processes are smooth, communication is clear, and unnecessary friction is removed. When barriers shrink, momentum grows. And momentum, Robert realized, is one of the most valuable forces in any program.

Barriers will always exist. But programs do not fail because they encounter obstacles; they fail because they fail to notice them. Robert's success came from naming, understanding, and systematically removing barriers.

Barriers (Application)

Robert used to think barriers were obvious. If something were in the way, people would mention it. If a process were broken, it would fail loudly. Over time, he learned the opposite was true. The most damaging barriers were quiet, tolerated, and absorbed by the people closest to work. Barriers do not announce themselves; they hide inside routines.

The Project Management Institute notes that programs often underperform because internal barriers are left unexamined and normalized over time [1]. Robert recognized this pattern immediately. The program looked functional from the outside, but internally, effort was being wasted compensating for friction no one had officially named.

So, he changed his approach.

Stopped asking, *"Why are these employees so unmotivated?"*

And began asking, "What are the barriers that are preventing us from reaching our goals more efficiently?"

That question revealed far more than complaints ever had.

Identifying Invisible Barriers

Robert began by observing rather than asking. He watched how staff moved through tasks, how volunteers navigated systems, and where people hesitated. He noticed repeated workarounds: duplicate data entry, informal approvals, and side conversations to clarify instructions. These were not inefficiencies caused by people; they were symptoms of structural barriers.

Workplace efficiency research shows that when barriers are embedded in workflows, individuals compensate by increasing effort, which temporarily masks system failure while accelerating burnout [7]. Robert realized the program had been surviving on compensation rather than design.

Categorizing Barriers to Reduce Overwhelm

To avoid being overwhelmed, Robert grouped program-specific barriers into four categories:

- Process barriers (unclear steps, redundant approvals)
- Communication barriers (missing or delayed information)
- Resource barriers (time, tools, or staffing mismatches)
- Environmental barriers (layout, access, or scheduling conflicts)

This categorization made barriers manageable. PMI emphasizes that breaking complex issues into defined categories improves problem-solving and prioritization [12]. Once barriers were named, they could be addressed deliberately.

Separating True Constraints from Self-Imposed Barriers

One of Robert's most important insights was that not all barriers were real. Some existed because "it's always been done." Harvard Business Review notes that organizations frequently mistake habits for constraints, continuing inefficient practices long after their original justification has expired [2].

Robert challenged assumptions:
- Does this approval still add value?
- Does this report inform you of decisions?
- Does this step protect quality, or just tradition?

Several barriers were removed once questioned.

Pro tip: removing a system after recognition of its ineffectiveness does not mean it must be replaced with another system.

Prioritizing Barriers That Matter

Not every barrier deserved attention. Organizational development research confirms that trying to remove all friction at once often leads to stalled progress [10]. Robert prioritized obstacles based on a 1-10 scale of three criteria:

- Frequency (how often it occurred)
- Impact (how much it slowed or harmed outcomes)
- Drain (how much effort it silently consumed)

Only barriers with a score of five or higher on at least one of those criteria were addressed immediately. Others were documented and monitored.

Design Solutions, Not Workarounds

Robert made a deliberate rule: no permanent workarounds. If a workaround was necessary more than twice, the system needed to be redesigned. This shifted responsibility away from individuals and back to leadership.

PMI emphasizes that sustainable programs reduce reliance on informal fixes and instead strengthen underlying processes [12]. Robert simplified workflows, clarified decision rights, and removed unnecessary steps. Each change reduced effort without reducing standards.

Using Feedback to Surface New Barriers

Robert also recognized that leaders are often the last to experience barriers directly. Organizational Behavior Institute research highlights that feedback systems are critical for identifying friction that leadership may overlook [5]. Robert created safe channels for staff and volunteers to name barriers without fear of criticism. Over time, people stopped quietly compensating and started speaking up earlier. This reduced frustration and improved trust.

Measuring the Impact of Barrier Removal

Barrier removal was not about comfort; it was about performance. Robert tracked what changed after barriers were addressed: time saved, errors reduced, energy restored. Organizational research shows that incremental removal of barriers produces compounding gains in productivity and morale [10].

Slight changes added up quickly.

Blueprint for the Reader

Robert's approach to barriers can be replicated:

1. Look for **workarounds**, not complaints [7]
2. Observe workflows to identify friction.
3. Categorize barriers to make them manageable [12]
4. Challenge habits mistaken for constraints [2]
5. Prioritize barriers that drain time, energy, or outcomes [10]
6. Replace workarounds with **system redesign**, not heroics [12]
7. Use feedback to surface barriers early [5]

Next-Step Growth Actions

Next-step growth actions bridge analysis and transformation. Leaders frequently get stuck in one of two traps: either they make plans so large they never start, or they make plans so vague they never matter. Robert initially leaned toward the first trap. His early growth plan resembled a corporate restructuring proposal more than a practical set of actions designed to help grow the organization. It included phrases like 'expand capacity significantly' and 'optimize program scalability,' both of which sounded impressive but meant absolutely nothing in practice.

The breakthrough came when he learned to ask a different question: 'What is the smallest meaningful improvement we can achieve?' This reframing changed everything. Instead of focusing on long-term aspirations, he focused on short-term momentum. Incremental improvements lead to greater long-term success than radical, large-scale reforms, because they are easier to implement, sustain, and adopt by teams [1].

Robert began identifying growth actions by reviewing three categories: capacity, quality, and engagement. Capacity growth included streamlining processes, improving training, and identifying new tools and partnerships. Quality growth focused on improving the participant's experience, simplifying instructions, clarifying expectations, and gathering feedback. Engagement growth included increased communication, strengthened community connections, and refined program incentives.

One of Robert's most successful strategies was the 'One Change Per Cycle' method. Instead of attempting to overhaul everything at once, he implemented one meaningful improvement per program, with the frequency depending on the issue's complexity. These changes included updating a form, revising the curriculum, clarifying staff responsibilities, redesigning a room layout, or improving the tracking system. None was dramatic, but each created a visible improvement.

Growth also depended on team involvement. Robert learned that the best ideas often come from those performing operational tasks. He began holding collaborative improvement meetings in which staff identified small barriers and proposed practical solutions. This approach not only generated better ideas but also built ownership, morale, and engagement. Compliance turns to collaboration when people feel their input matters.

Finally, Robert learned that next-step growth must be documented. Programs often improve but fail to record what was changed, how it was changed, and why it was changed. This leads to repeated mistakes, forgotten insights, and the loss of institutional knowledge. Robert implemented a simple growth log where improvements, reasons, and outcomes were recorded. This created a roadmap of progress and a reference for future decision-making.

In the end, next-step growth actions are about steady and reliable movement. This approach has been proven to be the best way to transform programs from functional to exceptional. Robert discovered that programs grow the same way people do, through consistent, intentional effort, taking one step at a time.

Next-Step Growth Actions (Application)

For Robert, growth used to mean expansion, more participants, more partners, more activity. Growth in his mind was synonymous with success, and any slowing down felt like failure. What experience taught him, often the hard way, was that growth without readiness does not scale impact. It scales dysfunction.

The Project Management Institute emphasizes that sustainable growth occurs when programs strengthen capability before increasing scope, rather than reacting to demand prematurely [1]. Robert had done the opposite. Demand showed up, and he chased it. The program expanded outward while its systems lagged.

Shifting Growth from Ambition to Readiness

Robert realized that next-step growth was not about ideas; it was about conditions. Growth required stability in staffing, clarity in communication, reliability in timelines, and confidence in safety systems. Without those, expansion simply multiplied existing weaknesses.

Harvard Business Review notes that organizations often fail during growth phases because leaders mistake momentum for readiness and assume systems will "catch up later" [2]. Robert recognized himself in that description. He had been betting on future fixes rather than on present preparation. He paused expansion, not indefinitely, but intentionally.

Identifying Growth Triggers

Instead of vague plans, Robert defined growth triggers, specific indicators that signaled readiness. These included consistent participation rates, stable staffing coverage, predictable timelines, and positive feedback trends. PMI highlights that data-informed decision-making improves growth outcomes by reducing risk and preventing premature scaling [12].

Prioritizing Depth Before Breadth

One of Robert's most important decisions was choosing depth over breadth. Instead of launching new initiatives, he strengthened existing ones. Organizational development research confirms that incremental improvements produce stronger long-term results than rapid expansion, particularly in complex human-centered programs [10].

Robert refined workflows. He reduced barriers. He stabilized communication. Each improvement increased capacity without increasing scope. Growth began internally before it ever showed externally.

Aligning Growth Actions to the Target Population

Growth also had to align with the program's target audience. Robert resisted opportunities that pulled the program away from its defined target population, even when they were well-funded or obvious. PMI's global research emphasizes that growth misaligned with beneficiary needs erodes impact and credibility over time [1]. This discipline protected the program's identity and prevented mission drift.

Sequencing Growth Actions Intentionally

Rather than launching multiple growth initiatives at once, Robert sequenced actions. Staffing capacity increased before participant numbers. Communication systems were strengthened before partnerships expanded. Timeline reliability was confirmed before new deliverables were added.

Research on workplace efficiency shows that unmanaged growth introduces barriers faster than teams can adapt to them [7]. Sequencing prevented overload and preserved quality.

Using Feedback to Guide Growth Decisions

Feedback became a primary input for growth decisions. Robert paid close attention to signs of strain: delayed responses, increased confusion, rising frustration. Organizational Behavior Institute research highlights that feedback systems reveal early indicators of overload that metrics alone may miss [5].

When feedback signaled stress, growth paused. When feedback showed confidence and clarity, growth resumed. This responsiveness made growth feel intentional rather than chaotic.

Defining "Enough"

The most challenging lesson was learning to define *enough*. Not every opportunity needed to be pursued. Not every demand required a yes. Robert knew that saying no was sometimes the most responsible growth decision available.

This reflected Jim Collins's principle that disciplined organizations grow by choosing to focus on expansion for its own sake [13]. Growth was no longer about scale. It was about sustainability.

Blueprint for the Reader

Robert's approach to next-step growth can be replicated:

1. Define growth as readiness, not expansion [1]
2. Establish clear triggers that signal when growth is appropriate [12]
3. Prioritize internal stability before external scale [10]
4. Align growth actions with the target population, not opportunity alone [1]
5. Sequence growth to prevent overload and barrier creation [7]
6. Use feedback to detect strain early [5]
7. Define what "enough" looks like to protect sustainability [13]

PART IV REVIEW

At the end of the program cycle comes the decisive moment: what worked and what did not. Document it and prepare to do it all again.

Additional Feedback Review

One of the most critical lessons Robert learned was that feedback evolves. When programs change, expectations change. When expectations change, experiences change. And when experiences change, the feedback that follows reveals new truths. The purpose of the ongoing review is not to prove that the last improvement worked, but to ensure that progress continues.

Robert implemented a quarterly feedback cycle that collected input from staff, volunteers, participants, and partners. He discovered that each group experienced the program differently. Staff focused on processes. Volunteers focused on clarity. Participants focused on comfort and structure. Partners focused on consistency and communication. Each perspective revealed something important and incomplete on its own, but together they gave a complete picture of the program.

Research supports the value of mixed-source feedback. Programs that gather input from multiple stakeholders identify issues more accurately and implement more successful improvement strategies [1]. Robert found this to be true immediately: feedback that looked negative from one angle made perfect sense when combined with feedback from another group.

One of Robert's most significant breakthroughs was learning to categorize feedback into three groups: actionable, informational, and emotional. Actionable feedback identified an area for improvement with a clear next step. Informational feedback offered insight without requiring change. Emotional feedback reflects feelings that are essential to acknowledge but need careful interpretation. Combined, this information provides a detailed view of the programs, systems, and daily operations.

This system prevented the team from reacting impulsively to every comment. Instead, they focused their energy on true opportunities. Robert also learned the importance of transparency. When feedback led to changes, he communicated the updates clearly. When feedback could not be implemented, he explained why. This built trust and limited frustration.

Finally, Robert recognized that feedback review is not just about finding weaknesses; it is also about identifying strengths. Additional feedback highlighted which improvements succeeded, which partnerships thrived, and which activities consistently delivered value. By reinforcing what worked and addressing what did not, the program avoids slipping back into old patterns.

Feedback review is not about perfection; it is about alignment. Programs grow when leaders listen with intent, make wise adjustments, and communicate clearly. Programs thrive when feedback becomes a rhythm and is organized appropriately.

Additional Feedback Review (Application)

Robert initially believed that once feedback was collected, reviewed, and acted upon, the work was done. What experience taught him was more subtle and far more critical: first-pass feedback only tells part of the story. The fundamental insight often lives in what emerges *after* the initial response. Programs rarely fail because leaders ignore feedback once. They fail because leaders assume one round is enough.

PMI's research on program performance emphasizes that sustainable improvement depends on continuous feedback review rather than single-cycle correction [1]. Robert realized that while his team had grown comfortable giving feedback, they rarely revisited it to see whether the changes worked over time.

Understanding the Limits of First-Round Feedback

Robert noticed that early feedback was often incomplete and nonspecific. Participants commented on what was most frustrating that week. Volunteers shared what was easiest to articulate. Harvard Business Review notes that organizations frequently misinterpret early feedback as comprehensive insight, overlooking delayed or downstream effects [2]. Robert began treating initial feedback as a signal rather than a conclusion.

He scheduled additional feedback reviews with follow-up questions to clarify the problem and then scheduled follow-up discussions after changes (if required) had time to settle. This allowed patterns to emerge that improved the program, and the people within the organization felt heard and confident in leadership's willingness to address issues.

Looking for What Changed—and What Did not.

In additional feedback reviews, Robert focused on comparison. What felt different? What stayed the same? What new issues appeared? PMI guidance emphasizes that evaluation is most effective when feedback is reviewed longitudinally rather than episodically [12].

Sometimes adjustments worked precisely as intended. Other times, they solved one problem only to create another. Without a second look, those tradeoffs would have gone unnoticed. This practice prevented the program from mistaking activity for improvement.

Identifying Secondary and Hidden Effects

One of the most valuable outcomes of additional feedback review was the discovery of secondary effects. Schedule changes improved attendance but increased staff fatigue. A new communication tool reduced confusion but excluded some volunteers. These failures would go unnoticed in most cases without this crucial step.

Organizational development research shows that incremental change often reveals hidden dependencies that only surface after implementation [10]. Robert learned to expect this and plan for it rather than being surprised. Feedback reviews became opportunities to refine or even reverse changes made.

Separating Adaptation from Backtracking

Robert also learned to communicate clearly that reviewing feedback again did not mean indecision. It meant responsibility. Learning & Development Quarterly emphasizes that transparent communication around adjustments increases trust and engagement, even when changes are ongoing [8].

Robert explained why feedback was being revisited and what he was listening for. This prevented fatigue and cynicism. People understood that their input mattered beyond the first conversation.

Using Additional Feedback to Detect Strain

Additional feedback reviews became an early warning system. Organizational Behavior Institute research highlights that repeated feedback cycles reveal strain patterns before performance metrics decline [5]. Robert listened to tone shifts, recurring comments, and subtle frustration. These signals allowed him to slow down, adjust, and refine expectations before problems escalated.

Preventing Overcorrection

One risk Robert learned to manage was overcorrecting. *Not* every repeated comment required a new change. PMI emphasizes that leaders must balance responsiveness with stability to avoid constant disruption [12].

Robert used additional feedback to confirm patterns rather than chase outliers. When feedback was inconsistent or isolated, he monitored rather than acted. This protected the program from oscillating unnecessarily.

Documenting Learning for the Future

Robert documented what additional feedback revealed. He made a list of what was changed, what worked well, and what did not. This created institutional memory. Over time, patterns emerged that informed future decisions and reduced trial-and-error.

People Analytics research shows that benchmarking improvement over time strengthens program evaluation and decision-making [11]. Additional feedback reviews became data points, not anecdotes.

Blueprint for the Reader

Robert's approach to additional feedback review can be replicated:

1. Treat first-round feedback as a **signal**, not a conclusion [2]
2. Schedule follow-up reviews after changes have time to settle [12]
3. Compare feedback over time to identify patterns and secondary effects [10]
4. Communicate clearly why feedback is being revisited [8]
5. Use repeated feedback to detect early signs of strain [5]
6. Avoid overcorrection by acting on patterns, not outliers [12]
7. Document learning to inform future decisions and benchmarking [11]

Programs do not stagnate because leaders ignore feedback. They stagnate because leaders stop listening too soon.

Robert did not improve outcomes by reacting faster. He improved them by listening for longer.

And once additional feedback became part of the learning cycle, improvement stopped being episodic and became cumulative.

Participant Follow-Up

Participant follow-up is how organizations evolve from good to great by providing the exact needs of the demographic they serve. Robert learned this when he saw that many participants who benefited from the program never stayed to take full advantage of the program's benefits. Not because they were unhappy, but because no one had built a system to continue the relationship. Follow-up is where impact becomes measurable, where trust deepens, and where programs transform from one-time experiences into ongoing support.

The biggest misconception Robert had early on was believing participants would return if they needed help or wanted more services. Research shows the opposite. Participants return when there is an intentional, structured follow-up system that keeps them connected and supported [1]. Without follow-up, programs operate like open doors with no invitation to come back.

Robert's first attempt at participant follow-up consisted of one email template and a hopeful attitude. Predictably, results were underwhelming. Some participants did not see the email. Some forgot the program existed. Some wanted to return but lacked a call to action. This prompted Robert to design a follow-up system based on predictable human behavior.

His first improvement was establishing a timeline-based follow-up structure: 24 hours, 1 week, 1 month, and 3 months. Each follow-up served a distinct purpose. The 24-hour message confirmed the participant felt supported. The one-week message checked for questions or barriers. The one-month message gathered feedback. The three-month message re-engaged participants with new opportunities. This rhythm kept people connected without overwhelming them.

Robert found that follow-up required multiple communication methods, including email, Phone calls, text reminders, automated messages, and in-person check-ins, and that, when used together, they produced significantly higher response rates. People respond to the channel that feels most natural to them. Robert's team created a simple rule: if it matters, use more than one channel. It may sound overwhelming at first, but remember to use small steps when developing solutions.

Follow-up also requires personalization. Participants responded best when messages referenced their specific experience, needs, or goals. Robert implemented participant notes and summaries of each person's needs. This allowed staff to tailor messages that felt personal instead of generic. Participants consistently reported feeling valued after this feedback system was implemented.

Another key breakthrough came from addressing barriers uncovered during follow-up. Participants often reported obstacles unrelated to the program, such as transportation issues, scheduling conflicts, childcare constraints, or confusion about next steps. By addressing these barriers early, the program improved retention and increased long-term engagement.

Finally, Robert recognized that effective follow-up created data. Tracking participants' responses, needs, and outcomes revealed patterns that would have otherwise gone unnoticed. These insights shaped future programming, improved outreach strategies, and demonstrated impact to stakeholders.

Participant follow-up is about relationship-building. It should focus on accountability, sustainability, and most importantly, the needs of clients. Robert learned that when programs follow up effectively, they stop operating as one-time experiences and become ongoing support systems. In the world of program management, that shift makes all the difference.

Participant Follow-Up (Application)

Robert used to believe participant follow-up was a courtesy. Something nice to do if time allowed. A check-in email here, a reminder there. If participants did not return, he assumed life got busy, or interest faded. What he eventually learned was more uncomfortable: lack of follow-up was not neutral. It was a message, and not the one he intended to send.

Silence communicates disengagement.

The Community Engagement Institute highlights that consistent participant follow-up is one of the strongest predictors of long-term retention and program impact [9]. Robert realized that while his team worked hard during program delivery, the moments *after* participation were ignored. That gap quietly undermined outcomes.

Recognizing Follow-Up as Part of the Program

Robert's first shift was conceptual. Follow-up was not an add-on; it was part of the program lifecycle. PMI emphasizes that programs achieve intended benefits only when engagement extends beyond initial delivery into reinforcement and review [12]. Robert saw that without follow-up, learning decayed and relationships weakened. Participants were failing to stay engaged because the program was not staying connected.

Designing Follow-Up with Intention

Rather than relying on ad-hoc check-ins, Robert designed a simple follow-up structure. He identified three purposes for follow-up:

- Reinforcement of learning or resources
- Assessment of participant experience
- Invitation to next steps

Each follow-up message was specific and included a call to action, whether it was a survey or an invitation to additional products or resources. Research on multi-channel communication shows that clarity and focus improve response rates and engagement [8]. Robert stopped sending long, multi-purpose messages that required too much effort to respond to. Responses increased almost immediately.

Timing Follow-Up to Human Behavior

Robert also learned that timing mattered as much as content. Immediate follow-ups felt transactional, while delayed follow-ups felt desperate. Community engagement research emphasizes that follow-up is most effective when timed to moments of reflection, not fatigue [9].

Robert standardized follow-up windows:

- A brief check-in shortly after participation
- A reflection prompt after some time had passed.
- A future-focused invitation once relevance returned.

This respected participant's rhythms rather than organizational convenience.

Using Follow-Up to Identify Barriers and Risks

Follow-up also became a diagnostic tool. PMI highlights that ongoing stakeholder engagement surfaces emerging risks before they impact outcomes [1]. Robert paid close attention to what participants said and what they did not.

Non-responses, vague replies, or repeated concerns signaled barriers. They mostly came in the form of confusion about expectations, difficulty accessing resources, and scheduling conflicts. These insights informed program adjustments far more effectively than assumptions ever had.

Avoiding Over-Follow-Up

Robert also learned restraint—too much follow-up created fatigue. Organizational development research confirms that excessive engagement requests reduce participation over time [10]. Robert intentionally limited follow-up touchpoints. Each message had a straightforward proposition: *Why does this matter to you?* Once this change was made, participants felt respected rather than managed.

Closing the Loop with Participants

One of the most significant changes Robert made was closing the loop. When participants offered feedback, they received acknowledgment, not explanations. Learning & Development Quarterly emphasizes that follow-up communication builds trust when participants see evidence that their input matters [8]. Even when changes could not be implemented immediately, transparency strengthened relationships.

Measuring Follow-Up Effectiveness

Robert tracked follow-up engagement: response rates, return participation, and referrals. People Analytics research highlights that benchmarking follow-up outcomes over time reveals retention trends that raw attendance data misses [11]. Follow-up became measurable without becoming mechanical.

Blueprint for the Reader

Robert's approach to participant follow-up can be replicated:

1. Treat follow-up as part of the program lifecycle, not an afterthought [12]
2. Design follow-up with one clear purpose per message [8]

3. Time follow-ups to participant reflection, not convenience [9]
4. Use follow-up to surface barriers and emerging risks [1]
5. Limit touchpoints to avoid fatigue [10]
6. Close the loop so participants know they were heard [8]
7. Track follow-up outcomes to benchmark retention and engagement [11]

Programs do not lose participants because people stop caring. They lose participants because the connection fades.

Robert did not improve retention by adding more reminders. He improved it by making the follow-up stylization meaningful.

Benchmark Data & Reporting

Benchmark data and reporting are the backbone of accountability in program management. While goals and activities create the framework for action, benchmarks provide a point to improve, continue, or stop, depending on the feedback received. Robert quickly realized this when he saw that most of his early progress updates relied on phrases like 'seems better,' 'feels smoother,' and 'I think attendance improved.' These are wonderful sentiments, but they are not metrics.

Benchmarking begins with identifying the right indicators. These are the measurable elements that reflect program performance: attendance rates, completion rates, participant satisfaction, engagement levels, turnaround times, and resource usage. Robert learned that good indicators are specific, meaningful, and directly tied to program goals. Bad indicators are unclear, overly complicated, or disconnected from the program's actual work.

The value of benchmark data is that it eliminates guesswork. Studies in performance management show that organizations using consistent benchmark reviews make better decisions, allocate resources more efficiently, and achieve higher long-term success [1]. Robert saw this firsthand when he began tracking baseline metrics and comparing them across weeks and months. With this data, Robert was able to categorize which systems were strong and which needed improvement.

Reporting is the storytelling side of benchmarking, turning data into insight. Robert discovered that stakeholders do not want spreadsheets; they want meaningful dialogue. They want to know what the numbers say about progress, challenges, and future direction. Effective reporting answers three core questions: What happened? Why did it happen? And what should we do next?

Robert developed a reporting rhythm consistent with the program's needs. Weekly updates covered short-term metrics. Monthly reports analyzed trends. Quarterly reports evaluated progress toward goals. Each report had a clear structure: highlight wins, examine challenges, interpret data, and propose next steps. Consistency builds trust among staff, partners, and stakeholders.

One benefit of benchmark reporting is that it reveals whether improvements are being made. When Robert adjusted the process or implemented a new system, the benchmark data showed the outcome quickly. This prevented wasted effort and ensured that energy was invested where it had the most significant impact.

Benchmarking also highlights where goals need to change. Sometimes the data shows that a goal was unrealistic; sometimes, it shows that a goal is too small. Flexibility becomes part of the strategy. Robert learned that benchmarks do not just measure progress; they inform future direction.

Benchmark data and reporting form the feedback loop that transforms program management from guesswork into leadership. Robert realized that programs thrive when leaders dare to look at the numbers honestly, interpret them accurately, and make decisions confidently. Benchmarking is not about proving success; it is about ensuring it.

Benchmark Data & Reporting (Application)

Robert used to treat reporting as an obligation, something done for funders, boards, or compliance checklists. Numbers were gathered at the end of a cycle, summarized quickly, and filed away. The reports looked professional, but they rarely influenced decisions. What he eventually learned was that reporting without benchmarking is documentation, not leadership. Quantitative data does not create clarity, comparison, or translation into qualitative information; qualitative information does.

The Project Management Institute emphasizes that programs improve performance when leaders use benchmarks to interpret results, identify gaps, and guide corrective action rather than merely recording outputs [1]. Robert realized he had plenty of data but no context. He knew *what* was happening, but not whether it was good, bad, or improving.

Defining What Should Be Benchmarked

Robert's first step was restraint. He stopped trying to measure everything. Harvard Business Review notes that organizations often overwhelm themselves with metrics, mistaking volume for insight and losing focus on what drives performance [2]. Robert identified a small set of indicators tied directly to program goals: participation consistency, completion rates, follow-up engagement, and workload sustainability. These became the benchmarks that mattered, not because they were easy to measure, but because they reflected real outcomes.

Choosing Meaningful Comparison Points

Benchmarking required reference points. Robert used three types:

- Internal benchmarks: comparing current performance to past cycles.
- Peer benchmarks: comparing similar programs or standards.
- Target benchmarks: comparing performance to defined goals.

People Analytics research highlights that benchmarking is most effective when comparisons are consistent and relevant rather than aspirational or arbitrary [11]. Robert resisted comparing his program to organizations that were vastly different. Relevance mattered more than prestige.

Turning Reporting into a Learning Tool

Reports stopped being summaries and became conversations. Instead of presenting numbers as conclusions, Robert presented them as prompts. What changed? What stayed the same? What worked and what did not?

PMI's guidance emphasizes that reporting should support decision-making by highlighting trends and implications, not just results [12]. Robert organized reports around questions rather than charts. Data became understandable—and actionable.

Identifying Patterns Over Time

Single data points became less important as the collective data enabled a more reliable view of the organization's overall health. Organizational development research shows that incremental improvement depends on tracking trends rather than reacting to isolated fluctuations [10]. Robert looked for movement across cycles, not perfection in one.

This prevented panic when a metric dipped temporarily and prevented complacency when one cycle looked strong. Stability mattered more than spikes.

Using Benchmarks to Surface Hidden Issues

Benchmarking also revealed problems that anecdotal feedback had missed. A steady decline in follow-up engagement signaled fatigue. A plateau in participation suggested timing issues. PMI notes that benchmarking can expose systemic issues that surface only when data is viewed longitudinally [1]. These insights allowed Robert to intervene earlier, before frustration became failure.

Aligning Reporting with Communication Needs

Robert also adjusted how reports were shared. Not everyone needed the same level of detail. Learning & Development Quarterly emphasizes that effective reporting communicates insights in formats appropriate to the audience [8]. Staff received operational information. Partners received outcome summaries. Boards received trends and implications. This prevented misinterpretation and reduced unnecessary debate.

Avoiding Metric Manipulation

One risk Robert confronted was metric distortion. When numbers become the goal, behavior follows. Harvard Business Review warns that poorly designed metrics encourage gaming rather than improvement [2]. Robert avoided this by trying benchmarks to learn. Metrics should be viewed as tools to identify potential areas for improvement but should not be the only means of analyzing effectiveness. Robert knew how to use the numerical data only as a starting point to get the bigger picture; he never acted on metrics alone.

Closing the Loop Between Data and Action

Data only mattered if it changed behavior. Robert built explicit connections between benchmarks and decisions. When benchmarks improved, successful practices were reinforced. When benchmarks slipped, targeted adjustments followed. This alignment reflected PMI's emphasis on benefits realization, using data to ensure programs deliver intended value over time [12].

Blueprint for the Reader

Robert's approach to benchmark data and reporting can be replicated:

1. Limit benchmarks to metrics tied directly to outcomes [2]
2. Use relevant comparison points, not aspirational ones [11]
3. Organize reports around questions and decisions, not charts [12]
4. Track patterns over time, not isolated results [10]
5. Use benchmarks to surface hidden or emerging issues [1]
6. Tailor reporting depth to audience needs [8]
7. Treat metrics as learning tools, not performance weapons [2]

Programs do not improve because they collect data. They improve because leaders interpret it wisely.

Epilogue

The hidden R... Repeat

If Robert learned anything on his journey, and if you have learned anything by walking alongside him, it is this: program management or business operations are not a straight line. It does not end with a perfectly color-coded dashboard or a performance report that makes your board high-five in the hallway. It ends with something far less glamorous but far more important: you do it again.

The hidden "R" in P.E.E.R. is Repeat.

Robert learned that the most significant danger in program management is not lack of funding, unclear goals, or even a broken copier (although that one tries its hardest). The real enemy is complacency, that moment when something "works well enough," and everyone quietly decides to stop checking on it. That is when programs drift, and progress loses momentum. But here is the good news: the opposite is also true.

Programs evolve when leaders keep evolving. Teams grow when leaders keep growing. Culture strengthens when leaders stay curious, humble, and hungry for improvement. The most successful programs in the world are not the ones with the most significant budgets; they are the ones with the strongest habits of continuous adaptation. As you close this book, here are the lessons to take with you.

- Clarity beats enthusiasm every time.
- Planning is leadership's compass, not its cage.
- The right partners matter more than the convenient ones.
- Small improvements done consistently build more momentum than big reforms done sporadically.
- Feedback is not criticism; it is a roadmap.
- Barriers shrink when named and grow when ignored.
- Growth happens in steps, not leaps.
- Review is the engine, but Repeat is the fuel.

Most importantly, you learned that leadership is not about perfection; it is about direction. Programs do not need flawless leaders. They need leaders who keep showing up, keep learning, and keep adjusting.

Do not stop here. Your program, your team, and your mission all get stronger every time you run the P.E.E.R. cycle.

Plan with intention.

Establish with structure.

Elevate with courage.

Review with honesty.

Then, repeat with purpose.

If you keep doing that, complacency will not stand a chance. And your growth will compound. The next chapter of your leadership journey begins at the end of this one, with the decision to keep going.

References

1. Project Management Institute. (2023). *Global Trends in Project and Program Management. PMI Publications.*

2. Harvard Business Review. (2021). *Why Organizations Fail to Identify Problems Early. Harvard Business School Publishing.*

3. Locke, E. A., & Latham, G. P. (2002). *Building a Practically Useful Theory of Goal Setting and Task Motivation: A 35-Year Odyssey.* American Psychologist, 57(9), 705–717.

4. Stanford Social Innovation Review. (2022). *The Power of Cross-Sector Partnerships. Stanford University.*

5. Organizational Behavior Institute. (2020). *Feedback Systems and Team Performance: Best Practices for Modern Organizations.*

6. Environmental Psychology Review. (2019). *The Role of Physical Space in Human Behavior and Organizational Productivity.*

7. Workplace Efficiency Consortium. (2020). *The Impact of Barriers on Workflow and Productivity. Annual Report.*

8. Learning & Development Quarterly. (2021). *The Effectiveness of Multi-Channel Communication Systems in Nonprofit Programs.*

9. Community Engagement Institute. (2023). *Participant Follow-Up and Long-Term Retention Strategies.*

10. Organizational Development Journal. (2020). *Incremental Improvement: Why Small, Consistent Changes Outperform Large Reforms.*

11. People Analytics Institute. (2022). *The Importance of Benchmarking in Program Performance Evaluation.*

12. Project Management Institute. (2021). *A Guide to the Project Management Body of Knowledge (PMBOK® Guide)* (7th ed.). PMI.

13. Collins, J. (2001). *Good to Great: Why Some Companies Make the Leap…and Others Do not.* HarperBusiness.

14. Project Management Institute. (2023). *Pulse of the Profession: Power Skills, Redefining Success.* PMI.

15. Lencioni, P. (2012). *The Advantage: Why Organizational Health Trumps Everything Else in Business.* Jossey-Bass.

www.ingramcontent.com/pod-product-compliance
Lightning Source LLC
Chambersburg PA
CBHW050656160426
43194CB00010B/1969